P9-DZZ-518

Horace Mann on

THE EDUCATION OF FREE MEN

———————

THE REPUBLIC AND THE SCHOOL

———————

CLASSICS IN EDUCATION

Number 1

Series Preface

This series presents the sources of the American educational heritage. There could be no more appropriate beginning than a volume of selections from Horace Mann's reports (1837-1848) to the Massachusetts Board of Education. As the commanding figure of the early public school movement, Mann more than anyone articulated the nineteenth-century American faith in education. His work still stands as the classic statement of the relation between freedom, popular education, and republican government

L.A.C.

THE REPUBLIC
AND THE SCHOOL

Horace Mann on
THE EDUCATION OF FREE MEN

Edited by
LAWRENCE A. CREMIN

LIVINGSTONE COLLEGE LIBRARY
SALISBURY. N. C.

CLASSICS IN

No. 1

EDUCATION

BUREAU OF PUBLICATIONS
TEACHERS COLLEGE, COLUMBIA UNIVERSITY
NEW YORK

© 1957 BY TEACHERS COLLEGE
COLUMBIA UNIVERSITY

LIBRARY OF CONGRESS CATALOG CARD
NUMBER 57-9102

THIRD PRINTING, 1960

PRINTED IN THE UNITED STATES OF AMERICA

Contents

370.4
M316 ✓

46726

The Republic And The School

LIVINGSTONE COLLEGE LIBRARY
SALISBURY, N C

Horace Mann's Legacy

By LAWRENCE A. CREMIN

HORACE MANN's political future never looked brighter than it did in the spring of 1837. Popular, influential, and universally respected, the able young senator could probably have commanded any elective office in the state of Massachusetts. Yet, when Edmund Dwight first approached him about becoming secretary to the newly-created State Board of Education, Mann's only responses were astonishment and disbelief. "I never had a sleeping nor a waking dream," he wrote in his diary, "that I should ever think of myself, or be thought of by any other, in relation to that station."[1] But Dwight, no man of idle words, persisted. Slowly, Mann's initial surprise gave way to the inner conflict and gnawing indecision which mark the turning points of a great career. By the end of June, the gifted lawyer had decided to trade a brilliant political future for an uncertain venture into the world of education. "My lawbooks are for sale," he wrote to a friend on July 2. "My office is 'to let'! The bar is no longer my forum. My jurisdiction is changed. I have abandoned jurisprudence, and betaken myself to the larger sphere of mind and morals."[2]

Few of Mann's friends saw any wisdom in his decision. They pleaded with him to reconsider, arguing that his political prospects "were not to be bartered for a post, whose

[1] Mary Peabody Mann, *Life of Horace Mann*. Washington, D. C.: National Education Association, 1937, p. 67. Other useful works about Mann include Raymond B. Culver, *Horace Mann and Religion in the Massachusetts Public Schools*. New Haven: Yale University Press, 1929; B. A. Hinsdale, *Horace Mann and the Common School Revival in the United States*. New York: C. Scribner's Sons, 1898; Louise Hall Tharp, *Until Victory: Horace Mann and Mary Peabody*. Boston: Little, Brown, 1953; and E. I. F. Williams, *Horace Mann: Educational Statesman*. New York: The Macmillan Company, 1937. See also the excellent chapters on Mann in Merle Curti, *The Social Ideas of American Educators*. New York: Charles Scribner's Sons, 1935, and Neil Gerard McCluskey, *Public Schools and Moral Education*. New York: Columbia University Press, 1958.

[2] Mary Peabody Mann, *op. cit.*, pp. 82-83.

returns for effort and privation must be postponed to another generation." What they could not know was that in
the largest sense, Mann's whole life had been a preparation
for this job.

Born in the little town of Franklin, Massachusetts, in
1796, Horace Mann grew up in an environment governed
by poverty, hardship, and self-denial. His body was early
strained by physical exertion, his soul tortured by the harsh
Calvinist preaching of the Reverend Nathanael Emmons.
Although he reports in an autobiographical letter that he
broke with orthodox Calvinism at the age of twelve (his
memory here appears to be incorrect; he was probably four-
teen or fifteen), the influence of his early training forever
manifested itself in the moralism of his intellectual and
personal temperament.

Mann's early schooling had come in brief and erratic
periods of eight to ten weeks a year, and from comparatively
poor teachers. Once he had learned to read, however, he
spent many an arduous hour poring over the ponderous
volumes of the Franklin town library, a collection of one
hundred and sixteen volumes given by Benjamin Franklin
himself in 1786. This self-education, when combined with
the fruits of a brief period of study with an itinerant school-
master, was sufficient to gain him admission to the sopho-
more class of Brown University in 1816. There his formal
education began in earnest, and he did so well at it that
shortly after graduation in 1819 he was invited to return
as a tutor at an annual salary of $375. For a young man who
several years before had found it difficult to raise $20 for
tuition, $375 was a great deal of money indeed.

It was at Brown, too, that Mann's humanitarian propensities began to come into full bloom. Apparently the inclina-
tion toward service rather than wealth had appeared very
early in his life. "All my boyish castles in the air," he once
said to a friend, "had reference to doing something for the
benefit of mankind. The early precepts of benevolence, inculcated upon me by my parents, flowed out in this direction; and I had a conviction that knowledge was my needed
instrument."[3] In the liberal atmosphere of Brown, his castles
found solid intellectual underpinnings. His papers before

3 *Ibid.*, p. 19.

the United Brothers, a literary society, are replete with reformist sentiments; and issues like immigration, temperance, and separation of church and state are resolved with a healthy republican bias. His valedictory address, on the progressive character of the human race, is a model of humanitarian optimism, portraying the way in which education, philanthropy, and republicanism can combine to allay all of the wants and shortcomings which have traditionally beset human civilization. How very much his thesis presaged the faith which was to sustain his later work!

For the more practical young idealist of 1819 there were two roads to success: law and the ministry. Mann chose the former. There was a brief period of "reading law" in the office of the Honorable J. J. Fiske of Wrentham, followed by an interlude of teaching at Brown. Then came a time of more concentrated study at Litchfield Law School, and finally, admission to the bar in 1823. Meanwhile, he had decided to settle in Dedham, and there his legal acumen and oratorical skill soon gained him the respect and popularity which in 1827 won him a seat in the state legislature. At thirty-one, the young reformer was well launched in his effort to do something "for the benefit of mankind."

For Mann, principle was always uppermost, and his legislative career was marked from the first by service to humanitarian ideals. His reformist sympathies, however, were never of the more popular Jacksonian variety. He had come to the legislature as a National Republican, and his temper was far too conservatively moralistic to cater to the crowd. His maiden speech to the legislature was a stirring defense of religious liberty; his second, in behalf of railroads, argued that the material prosperity deriving from good transportation would inevitably stimulate intellectual and moral attainment among the people. In 1829 he championed a public institution to care for the mentally ill; and the result was the state hospital for the insane, at Worcester, the first of its kind in the United States. From the beginning, Mann had displayed a vigorous interest in the temperance movement, and after his elevation to the state senate in 1833 he gave increasing attention to legislation regulating traffic in liquors. Throughout these years he also maintained a thriving legal practice, first in Dedham and later in Boston; and his reputation as a lawyer combined with his great personal charm to make him a favorite of the Boston intelligentsia. Of the many causes dear to Mann's heart, none was closer than the education of the people. While his actual teaching experience had been brief, he had long displayed a keen interest in more general matters of school policy, an interest which was widely shared among his more reform-minded colleagues. Nineteenth-century Massachusetts could boast a proud heritage of public education dating all the way back to the "Old Deluder Satan" Act of 1647. Yet during Mann's own lifetime, public penury and disinterest had allowed the schools to fall into disrepute, and there was talk that neighboring states like New York and foreign monarchies—yes, even monarchies!—like Prussia were outstripping Massachusetts in the quality and vigor of their public schools. The key apparently lay in the measure of centralization inherent in a vigorous policy of state support and concern for education. Sparked by Edmund Dwight, James G. Carter, Josiah Quincy, Jr., and the Reverend Charles Brooks, a reform movement arose dedicated to a similar policy for Massachusetts. An influx of reports on Prussian and French educational reform only quickened the imagination of these men. Discussions, consultations, meetings and memorials gradually paved the way for legislative action, and no one was much surprised when Governor Edward Everett—later to be President of Harvard—recommended to the legislative session of 1837 that a Board be created to further the cause of public education in the state. After failing initially to pass in the House, a bill authorizing such a Board was reconsidered and enacted on April 20, 1837. Two weeks later Dwight, who more than anyone else had lovingly presided over the conception of the Board, was dining with Horace Mann to urge his acceptance of the secretaryship.

II

The Board had been granted no direct authority over the schools; its primary function was enlightenment. Even the paid secretary was only to collect information about educational practice and publicize it throughout the state. If ever a post called for *moral* leadership of the first order, it was this one, and it is to Dwight's lasting credit that he persuaded Horace Mann to accept it. During his twelve years as secretary, Mann was literally indefatigable in the cause of public education. While actively serving the schools he was able to ponder their problems deeply and well. His twelve annual reports to the Board range far and wide through the field of pedagogy, eloquently stating the case for the public school and insightfully discussing its problems. The cogency of their analysis is measured by their striking relevance today; to peruse them is to consider some of the most fundamental problems of contemporary American education.

Public Education as a Moral Enterprise

Mann understood well the integral relationship between freedom, popular education, and republican government. The theme resounds throughout his twelve reports. A nation cannot long remain ignorant and free. No political structure, however artfully devised, can inherently guarantee the rights and liberties of citizens, for freedom can be secure only as knowledge is widely distributed among the populace. Hence, universal popular education is the only foundation on which republican government can securely rest. These Jeffersonian propositions he accepted as truisms which, by the 1840's, had been voiced so frequently as to be trite. For Mann, however, the problem went much deeper; it was essentially one of moral elevation. "Never will wisdom preside in the halls of legislation," he wrote, "and its profound utterances be recorded on the pages of the statute book, until Common Schools . . . shall create a more far-seeing intelligence and a purer morality than has ever existed among communities of men."[4] Knowledge was power, to be sure, but a power that could be used for good or evil. The essence of republican education could never be merely intellectual; values inevitably intruded.[5]

To raise the problem of values, though, was to raise other

[4] XII: 84. (The twelve reports will be designated here with Roman numerals. The editions referred to are those officially published by the State of Massachusetts. All of the reports have recently been published in a facsimile edition by the National Education Association and are obtainable at one dollar per report from the Senior Citizens of America, 1129 Vermont Avenue Northwest, Washington 5, D. C.)

[5] IX: 75 ff.

questions. Mann was tremendously impressed with the het-
erogeneity of the American population. He marveled at its
vast diversity of social, ethnic, and religious groups and
manifested concern lest conflicts of value rip apart the body
politic and render it powerless. Fearing the destructive pos-
sibilities of religious, political, and class discord, he sought
a common value system which might undergird American
republicanism and within which a healthy diversity might
thrive. His quest was for a *public philosophy,* a sense of
community which might be shared by Americans of every
variety and persuasion. His effort was to use education to
fashion a new American character out of a maze of conflicting cultural traditions. And his tool was the common
school.

Mann's school was to be common, not in the traditional
European sense of a school for the common people, but in
a new sense of a school common to all people. It was to be
available and equal to all, part of the birthright of every
American child. It was to be for rich and poor alike, not
only free but the equivalent in quality of any comparable
private institution. In it would mix the children of all
creeds, classes, and backgrounds, the warm association of
childhood kindling a spirit of mutual amity and respect
which the strains and cleavages of adult life could never
destroy. In social harmony, then, Mann found the primary
goal of the school.

Yet even social harmony was instrumental to the larger
purpose of social progress, an end closely tied to Mann's
limitless faith in the perfectibility of human life and institutions. Once common schools had been established, there
was no social evil which could not be attacked by their beneficent influence. Universal education could be the "great
equalizer" of human conditions, the "balance wheel of the
social machinery," and the "creator of wealth undreamed
of."[6] Poverty would most assuredly disappear as a broaden-
ing popular intelligence tapped new treasures of natural
and material wealth. Along with poverty would go the ran-
corous discord between the "haves" and the "have-nots"
which had characterized all of human history. Crime would
decline sharply, as would a host of moral vices like intem-

6 XII: 59.

HORACE MANN'S LEGACY

perance, cupidity, licentiousness, violence, and fraud.[7] The
ravages of ill health would most certainly abate.[8] In sum,
there was no end to the social good which might be derived
from the common school. "In universal education," he wrote,
"every 'follower of God and friend of humankind' will find
the only sure means of carrying forward that particular form
to which he is devoted. In whatever department of philanthropy he may be engaged, he will find that department to
be only a segment of the great circle of beneficence, of which
Universal Education is centre and circumference; and that
it is only when these segments are fitly joined together, that
the wheel of Progress can move harmoniously and resist-
lessly onward."[9] Here, then, was a total faith in the beneficent power of education to shape the future of the young
republic—a kind of nineteenth-century version of ancient
Athenian *paideia*. Little wonder that it could fire the optimistic American imagination to the extent that it did.

The Common School Program

Ideally, the common school would reach every child in
the commonwealth. Granted this opportunity unique in history, what would the school teach? For Mann, the answer
involved intellectual, moral, and political considerations.

Having read his classics well, he fully understood that
without literature men are savages, cut off from the wisdom
of the past and subject to the merciless vicissitudes of fortune. Intellectual education, then, begins with language, the
"indispensable condition of our existence as rational beings."[10] His insights into the teaching of reading and spelling are truly remarkable, for their own time or any other.
He sees learning as an active process in which "the effective
labor must be performed by the learner himself." He is
aware of the importance of motivation, noting that "until
a desire to learn exists within the child, some foreign force
must constantly be supplied to keep him going; but from
the moment that a desire is excited, he is self-motive and
goes alone." He observes that children can be "prepared"

7 XI: 87, 113.
8 VI: 56 ff..
9 XI: 135.
10 II: 40.

for reading by having interesting and inspiring stories read to them. He realizes, too, that a child's earliest words are learned as wholes; hence, the inappropriateness of beginning with the alphabet or syllables. On the other hand, he is far from doctrinaire about the system today called the "word method," for he also contends that a knowledge of phonics can be of inestimable value all through the teaching of language.[11]

While Mann is concerned with the mechanics of reading, he is by no means preoccupied with them. Throughout, his goal is precision of meaning and effectiveness of use, and his attacks on rote learning are sharp and unwavering. Furthermore, he knew enough to look even beyond this to the real questions of *whether* and *what* people read once they learn the mechanics of the skill. It should be no surprise that his *Second Report,* on language, was followed a year later by an eloquent—if somewhat moralistic—discussion of the function of free public libraries. Solemnly asserting the evil effects of literary trash on the popular mind, Mann saw in good libraries the key to an intellectual renaissance among the people. "Let good books be read, and the taste for reading bad ones will slough off from the minds of the young, like gangrened flesh from a healing wound."[12] In good libraries he saw the companions to good schools in the forward movement of the wheel of Progress. "Could a library," he concluded, "containing popular, intelligible elucidations of the great subjects of art, of science, of duty, be carried home to all the children in the Commonwealth, it would be a magnet to reveal the varied elements of excellence, now hidden in their souls."[13]

Language was the gateway to the subjects of the common school curriculum, and although there was some controversy about these, Mann was inclined to accept the usual list of arithmetic, English grammar, and geography in addition to reading, writing, and spelling.[14] The two significant additions he sought to make were human physiology and vocal music.

11 II: 44-52.
12 III: 94.
13 III: 96.
14 IV: 48-49; VI: 53.

For Mann, human physiology meant "an exposition of the laws of Health and Life."[15] He believed it was sheer folly that so much had been learned about the principles of hygiene and so little had been disseminated among the people. The social, economic, and moral benefits to the community from a universal program of health education would be legion. In the great work of education, he concluded, "our physical condition, if not the first step in point of importance, is the first in order of time. On the broad and firm foundation of health alone, can the loftiest and most enduring structures of the intellect be reared."[16] It was his concern for health, too, that led him to pioneer in calling for light, airy, and roomy buildings to replace the huts and hovels which were serving as schoolhouses in 1837.[17]

In urging the teaching of vocal music Mann showed surprising sensitivity to the aesthetic merits of the subject; indeed, he even gently chided his stern Puritan countrymen for being an "un-musical,—not to say, an anti-musical people."[18] Yet one senses that other arguments were uppermost in his mind. Thus, vocal music would promote health; in increasing the action of the lungs it would stimulate the circulation, purify the blood, and quicken the digestion. In fact, it could ultimately reduce the annual number of deaths from tuberculosis![19] Vocal music would mean intellectual exercise since all musical tones have mathematical relations. And finally—and with Mann inexorably—vocal music would have moral influences which would far transcend all its physical and intellectual utility. It could curb youthful passions and enhance classroom discipline; it could serve as the great tranquilizer of the young and the "grand mediator or peace-maker between men." One is somewhat overwhelmed by these grandiose arguments for a little singing in the schools. But Mann knew his Puritan audience well. He even took pains to point out that "the instruments of vocal music levy no contributions, upon another's skill, or

15 VI: 56.
16 VI: 160.
17 I: 27; III: 39-41; IV: 28-32; X: 64-68.
18 VIII: 129.
19 VIII: pp. 124-25. The influence of phrenology is quite apparent here. See pp. 13-14 *infra*.

our own money." They are indeed "the gratuity of nature."[20]

What is perhaps most important about Mann's view of the common school program is that he saw in it an educational purpose truly common to all. The common school would be ideally devoted to what we would today call general education. "The man is the trunk," he contended; "occupations and professions are only different qualities of the fruit it should yield."[21] Hence, the common school should *not* devote itself to specialized vocational training; such was alien to its purpose. Today, when these functions are properly assigned to higher rungs on the educational ladder, it is difficult to appreciate Mann's courage in taking this stand. He could easily have catered to popular practicalism by pressing for the introduction of apprentice programs; he did not. He was steadfast in his devotion to broader social purposes, believing, contrary to the classical philosophers, that true culture could be democratized and made universal.[22] "The development of the common nature; the cultivation of the germs of intelligence, uprightness, benevolence, truth, that belong to all;—these are the principal, the aim, the end,—while special preparations for the field or the shop, for the forum or the desk, for the land or the sea, are but incidents."[23]

In confronting the problem of moral education, Mann faced the question which was then central to the common school and has remained so ever since: What can be the moral foundations of a common educational program in a religiously diverse society? Mann himself was a deeply religious person. Yet for this reason above all others, he well knew that if any sectarian creed were made the basis of the common-school curriculum, the school would founder on this very point. Were Methodism taught, Baptists would withdraw their children. Were Protestantism taught, Roman Catholics would withdraw their children. And so on down America's long list of religious denominations. What, then,

20 VIII: 119.
21 III: 87-88.
22 I am indebted for this insight to Martin Dworkin.
23 III: 88.

could be the solution for an educator who saw morality as the ultimate purpose of the school?

Mann wrestled unceasingly with the problem, and as his years of office passed, he tended to embrace two solutions. First, he came increasingly to believe that certain common principles could be culled from the several sectarian creeds and made the core of a body of religious doctrine on which all could agree. For Mann, these were the great principles of "natural religion"—those truths which had been given in the Bible and demonstrated in the course of history. The fact that this new corpus of knowledge closely resembled his own optimistic, humanistic Unitarianism did not seem to trouble him. Nor did questions about "which version of the Bible" from Catholic and Jewish citizens. If the Word of God—personified in the King James Bible—were taught without comment, how could that conceivably be sectarian?[24] If the Fatherhood of God were taught as the foundation of the brotherhood of men, how could that be sectarian? Mann really raised these questions rhetorically, and the overwhelmingly Protestant people of Massachusetts seemed willing to go along with him, once he had fought and defeated the more vigorous sectarians among them.

The teaching of a non-sectarian, liberal Protestantism provided Mann's first solution to the moral problem. The other lay in a much more radical theory of moral instruction—one closely tied to Mann's belief in phrenology. Phrenology was a nineteenth-century theory which assumed that the mind is composed of thirty-seven faculties (for example, aggressiveness, benevolence, veneration) which govern the attitudes and actions of the individual. Behavioristic in outlook, phrenology also maintained that human character can be modified, that desirable faculties can be cultivated through exercise and undesirable ones inhibited through disuse. What a wonderful psychology for a social reformer! It promised that education could really build the good society.[25]

One of the outstanding phrenologists of the nineteenth century was an Englishman, George Combe. Interestingly

24 I: 61-62; VIII: 75-76; XII: 116-17.
25 See John D. Davies, *Phrenology: Fad and Science*. New Haven: Yale University Press, 1955. See also George Combe, *Lectures on Popular Education*. Boston: Marsh, Capen, Lyon, and Webb, 1839.

enough, Mann's diary reports that at the very time Dwight
was urging him to accept the secretaryship of the Board,
he was reading Combe's treatise, *The Constitution of Man,*
and finding himself completely convinced by it.[26] When
Combe came to the United States in 1838, Mann became his
close friend and disciple; in fact, some years later he even
named a son George Combe Mann. The influence of phrenology on Mann's thought is universally apparent. He freely
adopts its terminologies, assumptions, and propositions. Indeed, as John D. Davies points out in his study of phrenology, the *Sixth Report* "reads like a vast gloss on *The
Constitution of Man."*

The point here, of course, is that once the assumptions of
phrenology are accepted—and while phrenology as a psy-
chological system has long been discredited, many of its
tenets resemble those of modern learning theory, a case, I
suppose, of arriving at some good conclusions via a poor
theory!—one doesn't need to go far to argue that morals
can be taught outside of their historic context in particular
religious doctrines. Thus, *public*—or common—schools can
teach such publicly accepted virtues as brotherly love, kind-
ness, generosity, amiability, and others, leaving to home and
church the task of teaching the differing *private* sectarian
creeds which sanction these virtues.[27]

This key to the moral problem also provided Mann's clue
to solving the political problem. "It may be an easy thing
to make a Republic," he wrote in his *Twelfth Report,* "but
it is a very laborious thing to make Republicans."[28] The
problem of making Republicans was part intellectual and
part moral. "However elevated the moral character of a
constituency may be," he reasoned, "however well informed
in matters of general science or history, yet they must, if
citizens of a Republic, understand something of the true
nature and functions of the government under which they
live."[29] Yet implicit in the teaching of republicanism were
many of the same problems associated with the teaching of
morals. Whose brand of republicanism would be taught?
"It is obvious," he continued, ". . .that if the tempest of

26 Mary Peabody Mann, *op. cit.,* p. 71.
27 IX: 127.
28 XII: 78.
29 XII: 84.

political strife were to be let loose upon our Common Schools, they would be overwhelmed with sudden ruin."[30] Once again the answer lay in teaching those principles in the "creed of republicanism" common to all political factions: the separation of powers, the modes of electing and appointing officers, the duties, rights, privileges, and responsibilities of citizens, and the necessity of resort to ballot in place of rebellion. Principles which might engender strife and controversy were to be excluded in the interest of "commonness."

It is interesting to note that the principle of exclusion which appears to solve these problems itself raises other difficulties. When carried to its logical outcome—the omission of everything vigorously objected to by any segment of the public—it can leave a fairly lifeless curriculum. When the teacher arrives at a controverted text, Mann counsels, "he is either to read it without comment or remark; or, at most, he is only to say that the passage is the subject of disputation, and that the schoolroom is neither the tribunal to adjudicate, nor the forum to discuss it."[31] Whether this principle is a good one for a republican school is itself a moot question. Indeed, whether it is even a necessary corollary of a common school is also debatable. The dictum "when in doubt leave it out" will certainly avoid partisanship and controversy; whether it doesn't also avoid some of the most valuable things to be taught is perhaps the more important question. To criticize Mann, though, is not to argue away his problem, for it remains doggedly at the center of any effort to build a common school for a people of many religious and political convictions. It is only to contend that there are perhaps ways of teaching great issues which do not necessarily solve them once and for all, but which nonetheless enable students better to think them through and reach rational—if differing—individual conclusions.

Pedagogical Method

Much has been written about Mann's wisdom in the realm of pedagogical method. Indeed, one marvels at the

30 XII: 86.
31 XII: 89.

aptness and modernism of his ideas. The child is to be
treated with tenderness and affection. Reward rather than
punishment should be the propellant of instruction; mean-
ingful learning rather than rote memorization should be its
goal.[32] The influence of Johann Heinrich Pestalozzi is frequently cited as the source of these dicta, and correctly so.
Yet all too often the equally powerful influence of phrenology is ignored. Actually, both are important in understanding his pedagogy. It is significant, perhaps, that one of
the earliest books Mann read to equip himself for his work
with the Board was James Simpson's *Necessity of Popular
Education*.[33] A close perusal of that volume reveals that
for his theory, Simpson drew equally upon Pestalozzi and
Combe. Mann was undoubtedly impressed. Indeed, it may
well be that the oft-cited *Seventh Report,* embodying Mann's
enthusiastic observations on the Prussian schools, tells even
more about Mann than it does about Prussia. If ever an inspection confirmed what the inspector was searching for,
this was it. Even the most cursory study of Prussian education
in 1843 reveals much more there than met Mann's eye. Yet
the *Report* served well to advance his principles, even if
it did incur a sharp rejoinder from a number of prominent
schoolmasters.

Probably Mann's most penetrating observations in this
realm are his perceptions of the relation of technique to the
purposes of the common school. To begin with, he was one
of the first since Rousseau to argue that education in groups
is not merely a practical and financial necessity but rather a
social *desideratum*. The *Émile* had contended that the ideal
pedagogical situation is one teacher to one child. But even
Rousseau had counseled his readers to turn to Plato's *Republic* for guidance on mass education. Now here was Mann
contending by implication that the tutorial relationship
could not possibly serve the *social ends* of education. Only
in a heterogeneous group of students could the unifying and
socializing goals of the common school be accomplished.[34]

32 IX: 82-139.

33 Edinburgh: Adam and Charles Black, 1834. The volume was published in Boston in the same year. See also Mary Peabody Mann, *op.
cit.*, p. 85.

34 XII: 42-43.

Once this is granted, however, other problems emerge. A free society is concerned with individuals not masses; so is its education. How, then, can the values of individuality be reconciled with the necessity of teaching children in groups? Mann by no means solves this problem but, to his great credit, he recognizes it. He is one of the first to try to work out the pedagogical implications of a universal education for freedom. He counsels, for example, that children differ in temperament, ability, and interest and that lessons should be adjusted to these differences.[35] He argues that the republican school stands *in loco parentis,* and as such shares parental duties as well as powers. Hence, the school can no more dismiss a scholar from its classrooms—"unless temporarily," he tells us—than a parent can expel a child from his household.[36] Above all, he maintains, the discipline of a republican school is the self-discipline of the individual. "Self-government," "self-control," a "voluntary compliance with the laws of reason and duty"—these are the phrases he uses to describe the goals of true republican education. A blind obedience to authority on the one hand, and anarchy and lawlessness on the other, are equally unacceptable. The essence of the moral act is free self-choice, and insofar as Mann's ultimate purposes are moral, only in the long and arduous process of training children to self-discipline does he see the common school fulfilling its deepest commitments to freedom.[37]

Public and Profession

Mann's very first report maintained that Massachusetts would never get good common schools until public interest could be mobilized and well-trained teachers could be obtained. Both themes are persistent in the eleven reports that follow.

Although he was first a moralist, Mann's years in politics had served him in good stead. As a result, his success in arousing interest in the schools was unprecedented. Having convinced himself that education was the "hub and circumference" of the wheel of Progress, his cause became a cru-

35 IV: 50-53; IX: 101-109.
36 IX: 98-99.
37 IX: 93-94.

sade. Massachusetts was the battleground and public apathy, the foe. At issue were the future and fate of the nation.

Like any other crusader, Mann saw history on his side. The obligation to build common schools, he maintained, had been laid upon the people of the state by the founding fathers of the colony. "We can never fully estimate the debt of gratitude we owe to our ancestors for establishing our system of Common Schools. . . . Can there be a man amongst us so recreant to duty, that he does not think it encumbent upon him to transmit that system, in an improved condition, to posterity, which his ancestors originated for him?"[38] Building on the fact that the Puritan fathers, deeply committed to the preservation of learning, had at great sacrifice established schools in the wilderness, Mann conceived a historic tradition of education for freedom, a tradition which his own generation was duty-bound to perpetuate and strengthen.[39] Failure to do so would be a denial of its heritage. To him we can trace the time-honored link between the destiny of public education and the destiny of the Republic. From him derives the view that the history of American education is the history of the public school realizing itself over time.

Howard Mumford Jones, in a pungent—if somewhat overdrawn—characterization of Mann,[40] wisely points out that in his crusade for education, Mann promised something to everyone. He touched on the "hurt pride of the workingmen," the "pocketbook nerve of the wealthy," the "self-interest of the industrialists," and the "defensive response of the cultured, timid before the lower orders whose education somehow threatened the supremacy of Protestant humanism in the Boston Latin School." He warred against apathy in every quarter, assuring each segment of the public that its interests would be well served by educational expansion. Most curious of all, perhaps, is the fact that while

38 VII: 46. See also IV: 43-44; V: 68; VII: 193; and X: 108.

39 To be sure, the Puritans had established their schools for religious rather than republican ends; but this by no means renders Mann's argument irrelevant. See Samuel Eliot Morison's illuminating discussion in *The Intellectual Life of Colonial New England.* New York: New York University Press, 1956.

40 "Horace Mann's Crusade," in Daniel Aaron (ed.), *America in Crisis.* New York: Alfred A. Knopf, Inc., 1952, pp. 91-107.

his intellectual arguments had a radical tone throughout, they were addressed to groups that were politically and economically conservative. Indeed, those who uncritically accept Cubberley's classic "alignment of interests" showing "conservatives" in opposition to the public school movement[41] might well ponder the fact that it was a *Whig* governor, Edward Everett, who gave the Board life, and a *Democratic* governor, Marcus Morton, who in 1840 sought its elimination and a return to the "democracy of the local district."

Actually, the two great planks in Mann's platform were public support and public control of the schools. Public support he rationalized with a curious theory of taxation which was a kind of admixture of Christian communalism and utopian socialism.[42] Society, he maintained, is composed of successive generations of men. No one generation ever *owns* property; it merely holds property in trust, bound by obligations from the past and duties to the future. To fail to provide for the education which is the birthright of youth is crassly to violate this trust. It is little more than "embezzlement and pillage from children." Thus did the *Tenth Report* heap ringing denunciation on those who contended that education is a private affair, to be enjoyed by those who can afford it. True, this optimistic theory probably captured less interest from those who counted than did the detailed arguments of the 1841 report testifying that educated employees delivered more work for the dollar than the uneducated. Nonetheless, no one likes to be an embezzler—especially from children;[43] and more recent world events have demonstrated how influential ideologies can be, however bold or unorthodox they may seem.

As for public control, it was at the very center of the common school ideal. The obvious rationale was twofold. First, public control followed from public support; the public was simply interested in how its tax dollars would be spent. Second, only in control by the public as a whole could the danger of partisan control be avoided. Thus would the

41 *Public Education in the United States,* Rev. Ed. Boston: Houghton Mifflin, 1934, pp. 164-65.

42 X: 126-29.

43 I could not resist embezzling this quip from Professor Jones's essay.

"commonness" of the school be preserved.[44] Critical examination, however, reveals an even more fundamental relationship to the basic design of the common school. Public control—through the legislature, the Board of Education, local school committees, and other *civil* agencies—was the means by which the public could participate in defining the *public philosophy* taught its children. Thus was control of the school related to its ultimate purpose, which for Mann was always first and foremost moral.

A further problem bears comment here: the problem of centralization. One of the most important reasons for creating the Board was to counteract the adverse effects of local district control. Too often, district committees had seen their primary duties in cutting taxes to the barest minimum, no matter what the deleterious effects on education. Although the Board had the limited power of enlightenment, it was in many ways an agency for reasserting the historic control of the state over education. Yet no one was more aware than Mann that in local public interest, the schools had their greatest strength. In his very first report, he charged the low quality of public education to the "dormancy and deadness" of local communities. Qualified citizens were declining to serve as school committeemen; voters were not turning out for school elections. Teachers were pointing accusing fingers at board members and vice versa. "It is obvious," Mann wrote with crusading self-righteousness, "that neglectful school committees, incompetent teachers, and an indifferent public may go on, degrading each other, until the noble system of free schools shall be abandoned by a people, so self-abased as to be unconscious of their abasement."[45] For him, however, the answer lay not in the *substitution* of state for local authority. It lay in the invigoration of local interest. In genuine local concern coupled with state encouragement, he saw the key to good public schools.

Throughout his reports, Mann worked tirelessly to extend Victor Cousin's oft-quoted dictum, "As is the teacher, so is the school."[46] As Secretary of the Board, he presided over the establishment of the first public normal school in the

44 I: 43.
45 I: 46.
46 V: 38-64; VI: 39-42: VIII: 61-62, 69-74.

United States, at Lexington in 1839, and over the founding
of two others which followed shortly thereafter. He led in
the movement to set up teacher institutes throughout the
state. Indeed, no aspect of his educational work is more
important than his effort to define a "good teacher" and to
provide a flow of good teachers for the common schools.

"Teaching," he wrote, "is the most difficult of all arts, and
the profoundest of all sciences."[47] He saw the teacher as a
professional who had mastered not only the subject matter
to be taught but also the art of teaching. His *Fourth Report,*
discussing the competencies of "those who undertake the
momentous task of training the children of the State," is
one of the outstanding treatises of its time on the preparation of teachers. Mann begins with a truism which might be
boldly stated at least once each generation. "Teachers should
have a perfect knowledge of the rudimental branches which
are required by law to be taught in our schools. . . . Teachers
should be able to teach *subjects,* not manuals merely."[48]
In an age when teachers were all too frequently only one
jump ahead of their students—if ahead at all—the truism
was well worth repeating.

Knowledge of the subjects, while a necessary beginning,
was by no means sufficient. "The ability to acquire, and the
ability to impart, are wholly different talents. The former
may exist in the most liberal measure, without the latter."[49]
Thus Mann saw *aptness to teach* as a second great require-
ment of the teacher. This included the whole range of
techniques by which material to be learned could be ar-
ranged and adapted to the requirements of the learners.
"He who is apt to teach is acquainted, not only with common methods for common minds, but with peculiar methods
for pupils of peculiar dispositions and temperaments; he is
acquainted with the principles of all methods, whereby he
can vary his plan, according to any difference of circumstances."[50] For Mann, these were no mere "tricks of the
trade"; they were the very essence of teaching.

It is not surprising that Mann singled out for special com-

47 I: 58.
48 IV: 48.
49 IV: 51.
50 IV: 52-53.

ment the ability to manage a school. With all that has been written in the twentieth century about the "good old days" of the nineteenth, it may come as a shock to learn that not a year passed during Mann's tenure of office when he was not obliged to report several dozen cases of the "turning out" of teachers. This could mean anything from a simple "lockout" by the students to a genuine disciplinary insurrection in which the teacher was savagely beaten and thrown bodily from the schoolhouse. At a time when Mann was discussing school *teaching*, the tradition of school *keeping* was very much alive.

"Experience has also proved," he wrote, "that there is no necessary connection between literary competency, aptness to teach, and the power to manage and govern a school successfully. They are independent qualifications; yet a marked deficiency in any one of the three, renders the others nearly valueless."[51] He included under the rubric of "management and government" not only the matter of keeping order, but the whole area of grouping students in classes and the broader problems of motivation, encouragement, and punishment. For Mann, these were not minor matters to be "picked up" as the new teacher began his work; they were important pedagogical problems demanding the highest talents and worthy of the deepest thought.

Finally, he cautioned concerning the good behavior and pure morals of candidates for teaching. Pointing to the prodigious personal influence of the teacher on his students —an influence next in importance to the home—he noted that knowledge and technique would mean little if unaccompanied by character. School committees, he contended, are "sentinels stationed at the door of every schoolhouse in the State, to see that no teacher ever crosses its threshold, who is not clothed, from the crown of his head to the sole of his foot, in garments of virtue."[52] Where the supply of saints was to come from, Mann did not say. One wonders if he would have exacted the historic penalty against "sentinels" who fell asleep at their posts!

That Mann played such an active part in establishing the first public normal schools of the state is testimony to his

51 IV: 53.
52 IV: 59.

belief that good teachers could be produced through a care-
fully designed education. The role of this belief in the
emergence of a teaching *profession* is prodigious.[53] Much
has been written in recent years to the effect that teaching
can never be a profession because there is no special body
of professional learning to be communicated. To such criticism Mann's *Fourth Report* stands as an eloquent rejoinder.
Into the morass of pedagogical incompetence he projected
an ideal, one that for its time was a beacon and one which
still has a good deal of light to offer.

Public and Private Schools

Private schools had existed in Massachusetts for well over
a century when Mann wrote his *First Report*. Some were
maintained by churches as direct adjuncts of their religious
programs. Others were run as private ventures by individual
teachers. Still others—commonly known as academies—were
founded and conducted by self-perpetuating corporations
chartered by the State. Many had long and distinguished
careers; many did their work devotedly and well. What place
did these schools occupy in relation to an ideal which hoped
ultimately to embrace all the children of all the people?

Mann pondered the problem deeply and often, and there
is no doubt that he saw such institutions as direct threats to
the common school. One finds little in his writings about
private-venture schools. They were few; their function was
rather specialized; and their influence was limited. The
academies, however, were a different matter entirely.[54] They
attracted needed money from the public schools. Even more
important, they took the children of the well-to-do out of
the public school classrooms, rendering them "snobbish" and
"conceited" and depriving other children of their healthful
example. Finally, and most important, they took from the
common school the interest of the most influential segment
of the community. "The common school ceases to be visited
by those whose children are in the private. Such parents decline serving as committee men. They have now no personal motive to vote for or advocate any increase of the

---

[53] Mann was also quite sensitive to problems of social and economic
status in the emergence of a strong teaching profession. See XI: 94-99.
[54] I: 49-56.

town's annual appropriation for schools; to say nothing of the temptation to discourage such increase in indirect ways, or even to vote directly against it." [55] To make matters worse, the evil was self-aggravating. As public interest declined, so would school quality, and more children would be withdrawn by parents who could purchase better education elsewhere. Thus would the cycle continue until public schools were pauper schools, a disgrace to the community which sponsored them and the children who attended them.

As for private denominational schools, he was unreservedly opposed to them. He viewed such institutions as English imports, "in which children are taught, from their tenderest years to wield the sword of polemics with fatal dexterity; and where the gospel, instead of being a temple of peace, is converted into an armory of deadly weapons, for social, interminable warfare." [56] One could almost see the Reverend Nathanael Emmons behind each lectern in the caricature he drew of such schools.

How could these threats be overcome? For Mann there was one and only one answer: the improvement and elevation of common schools. He was realistic enough to know that as long as better education could be obtained elsewhere, people would send their children elsewhere. Indeed, he himself argued that a parent could not be expected to "sacrifice" his child to a visionary social ideal. If, after every effort had been expended to improve the public school its quality still proved inferior, parents had not only the right but the high obligation "to provide surer and better means for the education of their children." [57]

Mann never once suggested the abolition of private schools. He sought to win over their constituencies in open competition with quality as the test. Neither did he realize that quality is not the only test of a school, and that quality itself can be defined in many ways. While he was aware of status problems, he too easily convinced himself that parents would always choose better education over more exclusive education. The fact that some would always supremely value denominational bases for education seems also to have

55 I: 49.
56 I: 56-57. See also IV: 41; V: 67-69; and VII: 37.
57 I: 57. See also VIII: 51.

eluded him. Although his sympathies lay with the Abolition-
ists, one misses, too, the sense that common schools should
embrace all *races* as well as all classes and denominations.
While his faith that the common school would ultimately
triumph never wavered, he failed to grasp these problems
destined to dog his ideal in years to come. The difficulty
with moralists is that they sometimes see only straight ahead.

One wonders even more at Mann's failure to include
public higher education within his common school system.
At the very same time that Michigan's John Pierce was working out an educational ideal founded on universal education
and capped by a state university,[58] Mann was arguing that
the state's responsibility ended at the secondary level. "After
the state shall have secured to all its children, that basis of
knowledge and morality, which is indispensable to its own
security; after it shall have supplied them with the instruments of that individual prosperity, whose aggregate will
constitute its own social prosperity; then they may be emancipated from its tutelage, each one to go withersoever[*sic*]
his well-instructed mind shall determine. At this point, seminaries for higher learning, academies and universities, should
stand ready to receive, at private cost, all whose path to any
ultimate destination may lie through their halls."[59]

One can venture several explanations for his position
here. To begin with, there were many academies and colleges in the New England region which offered advanced
education of high quality for modest fees. By 1825, Amherst
and Williams had joined Harvard in Massachusetts alone.
And hadn't Mann himself managed to get through Brown
University without the help of either Massachusetts or
Rhode Island? In one respect, then, New England had a
long and noble tradition of private higher education which
Pierce was simply not confronted with out in Michigan. And
this may well explain the difference.

But everything points to even deeper reasons. Jefferson
once maintained that if forced to choose between universal
elementary education or a state university for leaders, he
would choose the former. Then, with characteristic Jeffer-

58 See *Annual Report of the Superintendent of Public Instruction of
the State of Michigan* for 1837, 1838, and 1839.
59 I: 56.

sonian inconsistency, he devoted his last years to building
the University of Virginia. Mann proved truer to his words
Throughout his career he contended that in a republic lead
ers could never far surpass the general popular level. Hence,
the important thing is not the training of leaders but rather
the education given the great body of the people. If the people are wise, the problem of leadership will take care of
itself. "By a natural law, like that which regulates the equilibrium of fluids, elector and elected, appointer and appointee, tend to the same level. It is not more certain that
a wise and enlightened constituency will refuse to invest a
reckless and profligate man with office, or discard him if
accidentally chosen, than it is that a foolish or immoral
constituency will discard or eject a wise man."[60] Throughout he was concerned with the greatest *general* proficiency
of *average* students. Thus it was never the remarkable progress of a few which captured his attention but, rather, the
more general progress of all.[61] By a doctrine of "first things
first," then, he gave himself fully to the problems of universal elementary education.

One can argue cogently that the midwestern ideal of
universal common schooling coupled with equal opportunity
for advanced education is more balanced, more complete,
and ultimately of greater benefit to the Republic. Indeed,
to read John Pierce's annual reports from 1837 to 1841 is
to wonder why he rather than Mann did not become
the father of public education as we know it today. On the
other hand, it is difficult to charge Mann's apparent disinterest in public higher education to opaqueness alone. His
arguments on the problem of leadership retain their timeliness, and are well commended to those who would perhaps
follow Plato too closely and err in the other direction.[62]

60 XII: 77.

61 See especially IX: 138-39.

62 It should also be pointed out in Mann's defense that in 1856, when
he was President of Antioch College, he served as one of a three-man
Commission which wrote a general school law for the State of Iowa.
Although the law was not adopted by the Legislature at that time, it
did conceive of a unified state system extending from the elementary
schools through the state university. See Vernon Rosco Carstensen, "The
History of the State University of Iowa: The Collegiate Department
from the Beginning to 1878," *University of Iowa Studies in the Social
Sciences, Abstracts in History* III, Vol. X (February, 1938), pp. 103-104.

III

Mann resigned his post in 1848 to take the seat of former President John Quincy Adams in the United States Congress. There followed a stormy period in which his Abolitionist sympathies projected him into the forefront of national politics. In 1853, after having been defeated for the Massachusetts governorship a year before, he accepted the presidency of Antioch College in Ohio, a new institution founded by the Christian denomination and committed to coeducation, nonsectarianism, and equal opportunity for Negroes. There, amidst the usual crises attendant upon the running of a new college, Mann finished out his years, succumbing to ill health in the hot, wearing August of 1859. Two months before he had given his own valedictory in a final address to the graduating class: "I beseech you to treasure up in your hearts these my parting words: Be ashamed to die until you have won some victory for humanity."

Mann had won his victory, and it only presaged other great victories to come. The public school soon stood as one of the characteristic features of American life—a "wellspring of freedom" and a "ladder of opportunity" for millions. Yet, as with the battle for freedom itself, victories are never final, and somehow today's educators find themselves fighting the very same battles Mann was supposed to have won over a century ago. Popular apathy and dissatisfaction, rising private school enrollments, sectarianism, objections to school taxes, a shortage of qualified teachers, disagreements over what a good teacher is, calls for special attention to the "gifted," and cries for harsher discipline—all of these problems of Mann's time have been raised anew. The cry is that times have changed, that a different America needs a different kind of school. Yet with all of the just claims of novelty, one cannot help but sense the continued timeliness of Mann's discussions. Areas of tension may change; for one generation it is religion, for the next it is race. Yet the idea of "commonness" at the heart of the public school remains ever pertinent. Similarly, while the specifics of the educational program may vary, teachers still must know what they are teaching as well as how to teach it. Amidst all the cries for a toughening of discipline, it is as true now. as it was then that one cannot train a child to freedom via the methods of slavery. And now as then, too, the charge of "Godlessness" against the schools is usually the cry of one who wants *his* sectarianism taught. It is this timeliness, perhaps, more than anything else that establishes the contemporary value of Mann's legacy. His writings continue to commend themselves to those seeking to penetrate the inextricable relationships between education, freedom, and democracy.

First Annual Report (1837)

Mann's First Report *sounds themes which are destined frequently to reappear in the reports to come. Four essential needs of the public schools are dealt with: good schoolhouses, intelligent local school boards, widespread public commitment to universal education, and competent teachers. In the following excerpt Mann discusses the corrosive effect of public apathy on the vitality of public education.*

Another topic, in some respects kindred to the last, is the apathy of the people themselves towards our common schools. The wide usefulness of which this institution is capable is shorn away on both sides, by two causes diametrically opposite. On one side there is a portion of the community who do not attach sufficient value to the system to do the things necessary to its healthful and energetic working. They may say excellent things about it, they may have a conviction of its general utility; but they do not understand, that the wisest conversation not embodied in action, that convictions too gentle and quiet to coerce performance, are little better than worthless. The prosperity of the system always requires some labor. It requires a conciliatory disposition, and oftentimes a little sacrifice of personal preferences. A disagreement about the location of a school-house, for instance, may occasion the division of a district, and thus inflict permanent impotency upon each of its parts. In such cases, a spirit of forbearance and compromise averting the evil, would double the common fund of knowledge for every child in the territory. Except in those cases, where it is made necessary by the number of the scholars, the dismemberment of a district, though it may leave the body, drains out its life-blood. So through remissness or ignorance on the part of parent and teacher, the minds of children may never be awakened to a consciousness of having, within themselves, blessed treasures of innate and noble faculties, far richer than any outward possessions can be; they may never be supplied with any foretaste of the enduring satisfactions of knowledge; and hence, they may attend school for the allotted period, merely as so many male and female automata, between four and sixteen years of age. As the progenitor of the human race, after being perfectly fashioned in every limb and organ and feature, might have lain till this time, a motionless body in the midst of the beautiful garden of Eden, had not the Creator breathed into him a living soul; so children, without some favoring influences to woo out and cheer their faculties, may remain mere inanimate forms, while surrounded by the paradise of knowledge. It is generally believed, that there is an increasing class of people amongst us, who are losing sight of the necessity of securing ample opportunities for the education of their children. And thus, on one side, the institution of common schools is losing its natural support, if it be not incurring actual opposition.

Opposite to this class, who tolerate, from apathy, a depression in the common schools, there is another class who affix so high a value upon the culture of their children, and understand so well the necessity of a skilful preparation of means for its bestowment, that they turn away from the common schools, in their depressed state, and seek, elsewhere, the helps of a more enlarged and thorough education. Thus the standard, in descending to a point corresponding with the views and wants of one portion of society, falls below the demands and the regards of another. Out of different feelings grow different plans; and while one remains fully content with the common school, the other builds up the private school or the academy. The education fund is thus divided into two parts. Neither of the halves does a quarter of the good which might be accomplished by a union of the whole. One party pays an adequate price, but has a poor school; the other has a good school, but at more than four-fold cost. Were their funds and their interest combined, the poorer school might be as good as the best; and the dearest almost as low as the cheapest. This last mentioned class embraces a considerable portion, perhaps a majority of the wealthy persons in the state; but it also includes another portion, numerically much greater, who, whether rich or poor, have a true perception of the sources of their children's individual and domestic well-being, and who consider the common necessaries of their life, their food and fuel and clothes, and all their bodily comforts as superfluities, compared with paramount necessity of a proper mental and moral culture of their offspring.

The maintenance of free schools rests wholly upon the social principle. It is emphatically a case where men, individually powerless, are collectively strong. The population of Massachusetts, being more than *eighty* to the square mile, gives it the power of maintaining common schools. Take the whole range of the western and south-western states, and their population, probably, does not exceed a dozen or fifteen to the square mile. Hence, except in favorable localities, common schools are impossible; as the population upon a territory of convenient size for a district, is too small to sustain a school. Here, nothing is easier. But by dividing our funds, we cast away our natural advantages. We voluntarily reduce ourselves to the feebleness of a state, having but half our density of population.

It is generally supposed, that this severance of interests, and consequent diminution of power, have increased much of late, and are now increasing in an accelerated ratio. This is probable, for it is a self-aggravating evil. Its origin and progress are simple and uniform. Some few persons in a village or town, finding the advantages of the common school inadequate to their wants, unite to establish a private one. They transfer their children from the former to the latter. The heart goes with the treasure. The common school ceases to be visited by those whose children are in the private. Such parents decline serving as committee men. They have now no personal motive to vote for or advocate any increase of the town's annual appropriation for schools; to say nothing of the temptation to discourage such increase in indirect ways, or even to vote directly against it. If, by this means, some of the best scholars happen to be taken from the common school, the standard of that school is lowered. The lower classes in a school have no abstract standard of excellence, and seldom aim at higher attainments than such as they daily witness. All children, like all men, rise easily to the common level. There, the mass stop; strong minds only ascend higher. But raise the standard, and, by a spontaneous movement, the mass will rise again and reach it. Hence the removal of the most forward scholars from a school is not a small misfortune. Again; the teacher of the common school rarely visits or associates except where the scholars of his own school are the origin of the acquaintance, and the bond of attachment. All this inevitably depresses and degrades the common school. In this depressed and degraded state, another portion of the parents find it, in fitness and adequacy, inferior to their wants; and, as there is now a private school in the neighborhood, the strength of the inducement, and the facility of the transfer, overbalance the objection of increased expense, and the doors of the common school close, at once, upon their children, and upon their interest in its welfare. Thus another blow is dealt; then others escape; action and reaction alternate, until the common school is left to the management of those, who have not the desire or the power either to improve it or to command a better. . . .

The theory of our laws and institutions undoubtedly is, *first*, that in every district of every town in the Commonwealth, there should be a free district school, sufficiently safe, and sufficiently good, for all the children within its territory, where they may be well instructed in the rudiments of knowledge, formed to propriety of demeanor, and imbued with the principles of duty: and, *secondly*, in regard to every town, having such an increased population as implies the possession of sufficient wealth, that there should be a school of an advanced character, offering an equal welcome to each one of the same children, whom a peculiar destination, or an impelling spirit of genius, shall send to its open doors,—especially to the children of the poor, who cannot incur the expenses of a residence from home in order to attend such a school. It is on this common platform, that a general acquaintanceship should be formed between the children of the same neighborhood. It is here, that the affinities of a common nature should unite them together so as to give the advantages of pre-occupancy and a stable possession to fraternal feelings, against the alienating competitions of subsequent life.

After the state shall have secured to all its children, that basis of knowledge and morality, which is indispensable to its own security; after it shall have supplied them with the instruments of that individual prosperity, whose aggregate will constitute its own social prosperity; then they may be emancipated from its tutelage, each one to go withersoever his well-instructed mind shall determine. At this point, seminaries for higher learning, academies and universities, should stand ready to receive, at private cost, all whose path to any ultimate destination may lie through their halls. Subject, of course, to many exceptions;—all, however, inconsiderable, compared with the generality of the rule,—this is the paternal and comprehensive theory of our institutions; and, is it possible, that a practical contradiction of this theory can be wise, until another shall be devised, offering some chances at least of equally valuable results?

Amongst any people, sufficiently advanced in intelligence, to perceive, that hereditary opinions on religious subjects are not always coincident with truth, it cannot be over looked, that the tendency of the private school system is to assimilate our modes of education to those of England, where churchmen and dissenters,—each sect according to its own creed,—maintain separate schools, in which children are taught, from their tenderest years to wield the sword of polemics with fatal dexterity; and where the gospel, instead of being a temple of peace, is converted into an armory of deadly weapons, for social, interminable warfare. Of such disastrous consequences, there is but one remedy and one preventive. It is the elevation of the common schools. Until that is accomplished, (for which, however, they ought to cooperate,) those who are able, not only will, but they are bound by the highest obligations, to provide surer and better means for the education of their children.

Second Annual Report (1838)

Most of the Second Report *is devoted to the subjects of reading, spelling, and composition in the schools. A penetrating discussion of the place of language in education is followed by numerous recommendations regarding the teaching of reading and spelling. Many are sensible; some are at best quaint. The following extracts include Mann's general discussion of language as well as a few of his more specific pedagogical recommendations.*

In this State, where the schools are open to all, an inability to spell the commonly used words in our language, justly stamps the deficient mind with the stigma of illiteracy. Notwithstanding the intrinsic difficulty of mastering our orthography, there must be some defect in the manner of teaching it;—otherwise, this daily attention of the children to the subject, from the commencement to the end of their school-going life, would make them adepts in the mystery of spelling, except in cases of mental incapacity. Anomalous, arbitrary, contradictory, as is the formation of the words of our language from its letters, yet it is the blessing of the children, that they know not what they undertake, when they begin the labor.

But, however deeply we may be mortified at the general inability of our youth to spell well, it is the lightest of all regrets, compared with the calamity of their pretending to read, what they fail to understand. Language is not merely a necessary instrument of civilization, past or prospective, but it is an indispensable condition of our existence as rational beings. We are accustomed to speak with admiration of those assemblages of things, we call the necessaries, the comforts, the blessings of life, without thinking that language is a pre-necessary to them all. It requires a union of two things, entirely distinct in themselves, to confer the highest attribute of human greatness;—in the first place, a creative mind, revolving, searching, reforming, perfecting, within its own silent recesses; and then such power over the energy and copiousness of language, as can bring into light whatever was prepared in darkness and can transfer it to the present or the absent, to contemporaries or posterity. Thucydides makes Pericles say, that, "one who forms a judgment upon any point, but cannot explain himself clearly to the people, might as well have never thought at all on the subject." The highest strength of understanding and justness of feeling, without fitting language to make themselves manifest, are but as the miser's hoard; without even the reversion of benefit, we may ultimately expect from the latter. And for all social purposes, thought and expression are dependent, each upon the other. Ideas without words are valueless to the public; and words without ideas have this mischievous attribute, that they inflict the severest pains and penalties on those who are most innocent of thus abusing them.

This is not a place to speak of the nature and utility of language, any further than is rigidly necessary to an exposition of the best mode of acquiring and the true object in using it. Within this limit, it may be observed, that we arrive at knowledge in two ways; first, by our own observation of phenomena without, and our own consciousness of what passes within us; and we seek words aptly to designate whatever has been observed, whether material or mental. In this case the objects and events are known to us, before the names, or phrases, which describe them; or, secondly, we see or hear words, and through a knowledge of their diversified applications, we become acquainted with objects and phenomena, of which we should otherwise have remained forever ignorant. In this case, the words precede a knowledge of the things they designate. In one case we are introduced to words through things; in the other, to things, through words; but when once both have been strongly associated together, the presence of either will suggest its correlative. The limited fund of knowledge laid open to us by the former mode bears no assignable proportion to the immense resources proffered us by the latter. Without language, we should know something of the more obtrusive phenomena, within reach of the senses, but an impenetrable wall of darkness would lie beyond their narrow horizon. With language, that horizon recedes until the expanse of the globe, with its continents, its air, its oceans, and all that are therein, lies under our eye, like an adjacent landscape. Without language, our own memory dates the beginning of time, and the record of our own momentary existence contains all that we can know of universal history. But with language, antiquity re-lives; we are spectators at the world's creation; we are present with our first progenitors, when the glory of a new life beamed from their inanimate frames; the long train of historic events passes in review before us; we behold the multiplication and expansion of our race, from individuals to nations, from patriarchs to dynasties; we see their temporal vicissitudes and moral transformations; the billowy rise and fall of empires; the subsidence of races, whose power and numbers once overshadowed the earth; the emergence of feeble and despised tribes into wide extended dominion; we see the dealings of God with men, and of men with each other;—all, in fine, which has been done and suffered by our kindred nature, in arms, arts, science, philosophy, judicature, government; and we see them, not by their own light only, but by the clearer light reflected upon them from subsequent times. What contrast could be more striking, than that between an unletterd savage and a philosopher,—the one imprisoned, the other privileged,—in the halls of the same library;—the one compelled by fear to gaze upon the pages of a book, the other impatient for the pleasure of doing it! As the former works his reluctant eye downwards over successive lines, he sees nothing but ink and paper. Beyond, it is vacancy. But to the eye of the philosopher, the sombre pages are magically illuminated. By their light he sees other lands and times. All that filled his senses before he opened the revealing page is only an atom of the world, in which he now expatiates. He is made free of the universe. A sentiment, uttered thousands of years ago, if touched by the spirit of humanity, falls freshly upon his responsive bosom. The fathers of the world come out of the past and stand around him and hold converse with him, as it were, face to face. Old eloquence and poetry are again heard and sung. Sages imbue him with their wisdom; martyrs inspire him by their example; and the authors of discoveries, each one of whom won immortality by the boon he conferred upon the race, become his teachers. Truths, which it took ages to perfect and establish; sciences elaborated by the world's intellect, are passed over to him, finished and whole. This presents but the faintest contrast, between the savage and the philosopher, looking at the same books, and, to a superficial observer, occupied alike.

To prepare children for resembling the philosopher, rather than the savage, it is well to begin early, but it is far more important to begin right; and the school is the place for children to form an invincible habit of never using the organs of speech, by themselves, and as an apparatus, detached from, and independent of, the mind. The school is the place to form a habit of observing distinctions between words and phrases, and of adjusting the language used to various extents of meaning. It is the place, where they are to commence the great art of adapting words to ideas and feelings, just as we apply a measuring instrument to objects to be measured. Then, in after life, they will never venture upon the use of words which they do not understand; and they will be enabled to use language, co-extensive with their thoughts and feelings,—language which shall mark off so much of any subject as they wish to exhibit, as plainly as though they could have walked round it and set up landmarks. . . .

One preliminary truth is to be kept steadily in view in all the processes of teaching, and in the preparation of all its instruments; viz. that, though much may be done by others to aid, yet the effective labor must be performed by the learner himself. Knowledge cannot be poured into a child's mind, like fluid from one vessel into another. The pupil may do something by intuition, but generally there must be a conscious effort on his part. He is not a passive recipient, but an active, voluntary agent. He must do more than admit or welcome; he must reach out, and grasp, and bring home. It is the duty of the teacher to bring knowledge within arm's length of the learner; and he must break down its masses into portions so minute, that they can be taken

up and appropriated, one by one; but the final appropri-
ating act must be the learner's. Knowledge is not annexed to
the mind like a foreign substance, but the mind assimilates
it by its own vital powers. It is far less true, that each one
must earn his own bread by the sweat of his own brow, than
it is that each one must earn his own knowledge by the
labor of his own brain; for, strictly speaking, nature recog-
nises no title to it by inheritance, gift or finding. Development of mind is by growth and organization, not by external
accretion. Hence all effective teaching must have reference
to this indispensable, consummating act and effort of the
learner. The feelings may undoubtedly be modified by external impressions, and, therefore, the mind is sometimes
spoken of as passive, recipient, adoptive; and the objects
around us have a fitness and adaptation to awaken mental
activity; but the acquisition of positive knowledge is not
effected by a process of involuntary absorption. Such a
notion belongs to the philosophy by which, a few years ago,
a grammatical chart was published and pretty extensively
sold in some of the States, whose peculiar virtue it was, that,
if hung up somewhere in a house, the whole family would
shortly become good grammarians, by mysteriously imbibing,
as it were, certain grammatical effluvia. The distinction
should become broader and broader, between the theory of
education which deals with mind as living spirit, and that
which deals with it as a lifeless substance. Every scholar, in
a school, must think with his own mind, as every singer, in a
choir, must sing with his own voice.

If then, in learning, all wills and desires, all costs, labors,
efforts, of others, are dependant, at last, upon the will of
the learner, the first requisite is the existence in his mind
of a desire to learn. Children, who spend six months in
learning the alphabet, will, on the playground, in a single
half day or moonlight evening, learn the intricacies of a
game or sport,—where to stand, when to run, what to say,
how to count, and what are the laws and the ethics of
the game;—the whole requiring more intellectual effort
than would suffice to learn half a dozen alphabets. So of the
recitation of verses, mingled with action, and of juvenile
games, played in the chimney corner. And the reason is, that
for the one, there is desire; while against the other, there is

repugnance. The teacher, in one case, is rolling a weight up hill, in the other, down; for gravitation is not more to the motions of a heavy body, than desire is to the efficiency of the intellect. Until a desire to learn exists within the child, some foreign force must constantly be supplied to keep him agoing; but from the moment that a desire is excited, he is self-motive, and goes alone.

Perhaps the best way of inspiring a young child with a desire of learning to read is, to read to him, with proper intervals, some interesting story, perfectly intelligible, yet as full of suggestion as of communication; for the pleasure of discovering is always greater than that of perceiving. Care should be taken, however, to leave off, before the ardor of curiosity cools. He should go away longing, not loathing. After the appetite has become keen,—and nature supplies the zest,—the child can be made to understand how he can procure this enjoyment for himself. The motive of affection also may properly be appealed to, that is, a request to learn in order to please the teacher; but this should never be pressed so far as to jeopard its existence, for it is a feeling more precious than all knowledge. The process of learning words and letters is toilsome, and progress will be slow, unless a motive is inspired before instruction is attempted; and if three months are allowed to teach a child his letters, there is greater probability, that the work will be done at the end of the time, even though ten weeks of it should be spent in gaining his voluntary co-operation, during the residue of the time. A desire of learning is better than all external opportunities, because it will find or make opportunities, and then improve them. . . .

When a motive to learn exists, the first practical question respects the order in which letters and words are to be taught; i. e. whether letters, taken separately, as in the alphabet, shall be taught before words, or whether monosyllabic and familiar words shall be taught before letters. In those who learnt, and have since taught, in the former mode, and have never heard of any other, this suggestion may excite surprise. The mode of teaching words first, however, is not mere theory; nor is it new. It has now been practised for some time in the primary schools of the city of Boston,— in which there are four or five thousand children,—and it is found to succeed better than the old mode. In other places in this country, and in some parts of Europe, where education is successfully conducted, the practice of teaching words first, and letters subsequently, is now established. Having no personal experience, I shall venture no affirmation upon this point; but will only submit a few remarks for the consideration of those, who wish, before countenancing the plan, to examine the reasons on which it is founded.

During the first year of a child's life, he perceives, thinks, and acquires something of a store of ideas, without any reference to words or letters. After this, the wonderful faculty of language begins to develop itself. Children then utter words,—the names of objects around them,—as whole sounds, and without any conception of the letters of which those words are composed. In speaking the word "apple," for instance, young children think no more of the Roman letters, which spell it, than, in eating the fruit, they think of the chemical ingredients,—the oxygen, hydrogen, and carbon,—which compose it. Hence, presenting them with the alphabet, is giving them what they never saw, heard, or thought of before. It is as new as algebra, and to the eye, not very unlike it. But printed names of known things are the signs of sounds which their ears have been accustomed to hear, and their organs of speech to utter, and which may excite agreeable feelings and associations, by reminding them of the objects named. When put to learning the letters of the alphabet first, the child has no acquaintance with them, either by the eye, the ear, the tongue, or the mind; but if put to learning familiar words first, he already knows them by the ear, the tongue, and the mind, while his eye only is unacquainted with them. He is thus introduced to a stranger, through the medium of old acquaintances. It can hardly be doubted, therefore, that a child would learn to name any twenty-six familiar words, much sooner than the twenty-six unknown, unheard and unthought of letters of the alphabet.

For another reason, the rapidity of acquisition will be greater, if words are taught before letters. To learn the words signifying objects, qualities, actions, with which the child is familiar, turns his attention to those objects, if present, or revives the idea of them, if absent, and thus they may be made the source of great interest and pleasure. We all know, that the ease with which any thing is learned and the length of time it is remembered, are in the direct ratio of the vividness of the pleasurable emotions, which enliven the acquisition. . . .

But one thing should be insisted upon, *from* the beginning, and especially *at* the beginning. No word should be taught, whose meaning is not understood. The teacher should not count out words, faster than ideas. The foundation of the habit should be laid, in the reading of the very first lesson, of regarding words as the names of things; as belonging to something else, and as nothing by themselves. They should be looked at, as a medium, and not as an end. It is as senseless for a child to stop at the sign of the printed word, in reading, as it would be to stop at the sound of the spoken word, in conversation. What child would not repel the intercourse of a person, who spoke to him only words, of which he knew nothing? No personal charms would be long sufficient to compensate for speaking to a child, in an unknown tongue. How is it possible then, that an active-minded child should not disdain the dreary pages of a book, which awaken no thought or emotion within him;— which are neither beauty to the eye, nor music to the ear, nor sense to the understanding? As reading is usually taught, the child does not come into communication with his lesson, by any one of all his faculties. When a child looks into a mirror, or at a picture where the perspective is strikingly marked, he will reach around to look behind the mirror, or behind the picture, in hope of finding the objects in the place where they appear to be. He cares nothing for the mirror, nor for the canvas;—his mind is with the things presented to his senses. In reading, the page should be only as the mirror or picture, through which objects are beheld. Thus there would be far more delight in looking at the former, than at the latter; because words can present more circumstances of variety, beauty, life, amplitude, than any reflecting surface or dead picture. Should we not revolt at the tyranny of being obliged to pore, day after day, upon the outer darkness of a Chinese manuscript? But if the words are not understood, the more regular formation of the Chinese characters gives them a decided advantage over our own letters. Give a child two glasses, precisely similar in every respect, except that one shall be opaque, the other a magnifier. Through the former nothing can be seen, and it therefore degenerates into a bauble; but the latter seems to create a thousand new and brilliant objects, and hence he is enamored of its quality. There is precisely the same difference in the presentation of words. Yet we punish children, because they do not master words, without any regard to their being understood.

But how can this plan be executed? In this way. During the first year of a child's life, before the faculty of speech is developed,—before he has ever uttered a word,—he has obtained a considerable stock of ideas, respecting objects, qualities and motions. During the next year or two and before it is usual to teach letters, he is employed through every waking hour, both in learning the words, expressive of known phenomena and also in acquiring a knowledge of new things and events; so that before the age of four or even three years, the items of his inventory of elementary knowledge swell to thousands. In his memory, are not merely playthings, but catalogues of furniture, food, dress, insects, animals, vehicles, objects in natural scenery, divisions of time, and so forth, with various motions and appearances, belonging to them all. Numbers, sounds, events, feelings, also come into the list. This is a stock not readily exhausted. By first teaching the names or phrases expressive of these, the substance is always present to his mind, and the words are mere signs_or incidents; and a habit is formed of always keeping the mind, in after-life, intent upon things and their relations,—a habit of inestimable value and the only foundation of intellectual greatness. . . .

Reading is divisible into two parts. It consists of the *mechanical,* and the *mental.* The mechanical part is the utterance of the articulate sounds of a language, on inspecting its written or printed signs. It is called mechanical, because the operation closely resembles that of a machine, which may receive the best of materials and run through a thousand parcels of them every year;—the machine itself remaining just as bare and naked at the end of the year, as it was at the beginning. On the other hand, one portion of the mental part of reading consists in a reproduction in the mind of the reader of whatever was in the mind of the author; so that whether the author describes atoms or worlds, narrates the history of individuals or nations, kindles into sublimity, or melts in pathos,—whatever was in the author's mind starts into sudden existence in the reader's mind, as nearly as their different mental constitutions will allow. An example of the purely mechanical part is exhibited in reading a foreign language, no word of which is understood; as in the case of Milton's daughters, who read the dead languages to their blind father;—they, with eyes, seeing nothing but black marks upon white paper, he, without eyes, surveying material and spiritual worlds,—at once charmed by their beauties, and instructed by their wisdom.

With the mental part, then, reading becomes the noblest instrument of wisdom; without it, it is the most despicable part of folly and worthlessness. Beforehand, it would seem quite as incredible, that any person should compel children to go through with the barren forms of reading, without ideas; as to make them perform all the motions of eating, without food. The body would not dwindle under the latter, more certainly, than the mind, under the former. The inevitable consequences are, that all the delight of acquisition is foregone; the reward which nature bestows upon the activity of the faculties is forfeited,—a reward which is richer than all prizes and more efficient than all chastisement;— and an inveterate habit is formed of dissociating thought and language. "Understandest thou what thou readest?" therefore, is a question quite as apposite when put by a teacher to a child in his horn book, as when asked by an Apostle of the ambassador of a Queen....

Third Annual Report (1839)

The Third Report *deals principally with the need for free public libraries as adjuncts to the public schools. Mann saw the power to read unaccompanied by a supply of worthy reading matter as an anomaly, "for with no books to read, the power of reading will be useless, and with bad books to read, the consequences will be as much worse than ignorance, as wisdom is better." His solution lay in the establishment of a free circulating library in every school district of the state. Only thus did he see the work of public education properly continued and complemented.*

Fourth Annual Report (1840)

Mann treated a variety of subjects in his Fourth Report, *among them schoolhouses, the need to consolidate overly small school districts, private schools, and attendance and disciplinary problems. He also included a thoughtful discussion of the qualifications of teachers, from which the following paragraphs are excerpted.*

A brief consideration of a few of the qualifications essential to those who undertake the momentous task of training the children of the State, will help us to decide the question, whether the complaints of the committees, in regard to the incompetency of teachers, are captious and unfounded; or whether they proceed from enlightened conceptions of the

44

nature of their duties and office, and therefore require measures to supply the deficiency.

1st. A KNOWLEDGE OF COMMON-SCHOOL STUDIES.—Teachers should have a perfect knowledge of the rudimental branches which are required by law to be taught in our schools. They should understand, not only the rules, which have been prepared as guides for the unlearned, but also the principles on which the rules are founded,—those principles which lie beneath the rules, and supersede them in practice; and from which, should the rules be lost, they could be framed anew. Teachers should be able to teach *subjects,* not manuals merely.

This knowledge should not only be thorough and critical, but it should be always ready, at command, for every exigency,—familiar like the alphabet, so that, as occasion requires, it will rise up in the mind instantaneously, and not need to be studied out, with labor and delay. . . .

However much other knowledge a teacher may possess, it is no equivalent for a mastership in the rudiments. It is not more true in architecture, than in education, that the value of the work, in every upper layer, depends upon the solidity of all beneath it. The leading, prevailing defect in the intellectual department of our schools, is a want of thoroughness,—a proneness to be satisfied with a verbal memory of rules, instead of a comprehension of principles,—with a knowledge of the names of things, instead of a knowledge of the things themselves;—or, if some knowledge of the things is gained, it is too apt to be a knowledge of them as isolated facts, and unaccompained by a knowledge of the relations, which subsist between them, and bind them into a scientific whole. That knowledge is hardly worthy of the name, which stops with things, as individuals, without understanding the relations, existing between them. The latter constitutes indefinitely the greater part of all human knowledge. For instance, all the problems of plane geometry, by which heights and distances are measured, and the contents of areas and cubes ascertained, are based upon a few simple definitions, which can be committed to memory by any child in half a day. With the exception of the comets, whose number is not known, there are but thirty bodies in the whole solar system. Yet, on the relations which subsist between these thirty individual bodies, is built the stupendous science of astronomy. How worthless is the astronomical knowledge which stops with committing to memory thirty names! . . .

2nd. APTNESS TO TEACH. The next principal qualification in a teacher is the *art of teaching*. This is happily expressed in the common phrase, *aptness to teach,* which in a few words, comprehends many particulars. The ability to acquire, and the ability to impart, are wholly different talents. The former may exist in the most liberal measure, without the latter. It was a remark of Lord Bacon, that "the art of well-delivering the knowledge we possess is among the secrets, left to be discovered by future generations." Dr. Watts says, "there are some very learned men, who know much themselves, but who have not the talent of communicating their knowledge." Indeed, this fact is not now questioned by any intelligent educationist. Hence we account for the frequent complaints of the committees, that those teachers who had sustained an examination, in an acceptable manner, failed in the school room, through a want of facility in communicating what they knew. The ability to acquire is the power of understanding the subject-matter of investigation. Aptness to teach involves the power of perceiving how far a scholar understands the subject-matter to be learned, and what, in the natural order, is the next step he is to take. It involves the power of discovering and of solving at the time, the exact difficulty, by which the learner is embarrassed. The removal of a slight impediment, the drawing aside of the thinnest veil, which happens to divert his steps, or obscure his vision, is worth more to him, than volumes of lore on collateral subjects. How much does the pupil comprehend of the subject? What should his next step be? Is his mind looking towards a truth or an error? The answer to these questions must be intuitive, in the person who is apt to teach. As a dramatic writer throws himself, successively, into the characters of the drama he is composing, that he may express the ideas and emotions, peculiar to each; so the mind of a teacher should migrate, as it were, into those of his pupils, to discover what they know and feel and need; and then, supplying from his own stock, what they require, he should reduce it to such a form, and bring it within such a distance, that they can reach out and seize and appropriate it. He should never forget that intellectual truths are naturally adapted to give intellectual pleasure; and that, by leading the minds of his pupils onward to such a position in relation to these truths, that they themselves can discover them, he secures to them the natural reward of a new pleasure with every new discovery, which is one of the strongest, as well as most appropriate incitements to future exertion.

Aptness to teach includes the presentation of the different parts of a subject, in a natural order. If a child is told that the globe is about twenty-five thousand miles in circumference, before he has any conception of the length of a mile, or of the number of units in a thousand, the statement is not only utterly useless as an act of instruction, but it will probably prevent him, ever afterwards, from gaining an adequate idea of the subject. The novelty will be gone, and yet the fact unknown. Besides, a systematic acquisition of a subject knits all parts of it together, so that they will be longer retained and more easily recalled. To acquire a few of the facts, gives us fragments only;—and even to master all the facts, but to obtain them promiscuously, leaves what is acquired so unconnected and loose, that any part of it may be jostled out of its place and lost, or remain only to mislead.

Aptness to teach, in fine, embraces a knowledge of methods and processes. These are indefinitely various. Some are adapted to accomplish their object in an easy and natural manner; others in a toilsome and circuitous one;—others, again, may accomplish the object at which they aim, with certainty and despatch, but secure it by inflicting deep and lasting injuries upon the social and moral sentiments. We are struck with surprise, on learning, that, but a few centuries since, the feudal barons of Scotland, in running out the lines around their extensive domains, used to take a party of boys, and whip them, at the different posts and land-marks, in order to give them a retentive memory, as witnesses, in case of future litigation or dispute. Though this might give them a vivid recollection of localities, yet it would hardly improve their ideas of justice, or propitiate them to bear true testimony in favor of the chastiser. But do not those, who have no aptness to teach, sometimes accomplish their objects by a kindred method?

He who is apt to teach is acquainted, not only with common methods for common minds, but with peculiar methods for pupils of peculiar dispositions and temperaments; and he is acquainted with the principles of all methods, whereby he can vary his plan, according to any difference of circumstances. The statement has been sometimes made, that it is the object of Normal Schools to subject all teachers to one, inflexible, immutable course of instruction. Nothing could be more erroneous, for one of the great objects is, to give them a knowledge of modes, as various as the diversity of cases that may arise,—that like a skilful pilot, they may not only see the haven for which they are to steer, but know every bend in the channel that leads to it. No one is so poor in resources for difficult emergencies as they may arise, as he whose knowledge of methods is limited to the one in which he happened to be instructed. It is in this way that rude nations go on for indefinite periods, imitating what they have seen, and teaching only as they were taught.

3d. MANAGEMENT, GOVERNMENT, AND DISCIPLINE OF A SCHOOL.—Experience has also proved, that there is no necessary connection between literary competency, aptness to teach, and the power to manage and govern a school successfully. They are independent qualifications; yet a marked deficiency in any one of the three, renders the others nearly valueless. In regard to the ordinary management or administration of a school, how much judgment is demanded in the organization of classes, so that no scholar shall either be clogged and retarded, or hurried forward with injudicious speed, by being matched with an unequal yoke-fellow. Great discretion is necessary in the assignment of lessons, in order to avoid, on the one hand, such shortness in the tasks, as allows time to be idle; and, on the other, such over-assignments, as render thoroughness and accuracy impracticable, and thereby so habituate the pupil to mistakes and imperfections, that he cares little or nothing about committing them. Lessons, as far as it is possible, should be so adjusted to the capacity of the scholar, that there should be no failure in a recitation, not occasioned by culpable neglect. The sense of shame, or of regret for ignorance, can never be made exquisitely keen, if the lessons given are so long, or so difficult, as to make failures frequent. When "bad marks," as they are called, against a scholar, become common, they not only lose their salutary force, but every addition to them debases his character, and carries him through a regular course of training, which prepares him to follow in the footsteps of those convicts, who are so often condemned, that at length they care nothing for the ignominy of the sentence. Yet all this may be the legitimate consequence of being unequally mated, or injudiciously tasked. It is a sad sight in any school, to see a pupil marked for a deficiency, without any blush of shame, or sign of guilt; and it is never done with impunity to his moral character.

The preservation of order, together with the proper despatch of business, requires a mean, between the too much and the too little, in all the evolutions of the school, which it is difficult to hit. When classes leave their seats for the recitation-stand, and return to them again, or when the different sexes have a recess, or the hour of intermission arrives;—if there be not some order and succession of movement, the school will be temporarily converted into a promiscuous rabble, giving both the temptation and the opportunity for committing every species of indecorum and aggression. In order to prevent confusion, on the other hand, the operations of the school may be conducted with such military formality and procrastination;—the second scholar not being allowed to leave his seat, until the first has reached the door, or the place of recitation, and each being made to walk on tiptoe to secure silence,—that a substantial part of every school session will be wasted, in the wearisome pursuit of an object worth nothing when obtained.

When we reflect, how many things are to be done each half day, and how short a time is allotted for their performance, the necessity of system in regard to all the operations of the school, will be apparent. System compacts labor; and when the hand is to be turned to an almost endless variety of particulars, if system does not preside over the whole series of movements, the time allotted to each will be spent in getting ready to perform it. With lessons to set; with so many classes to hear; with difficulties to explain; with the studious to be assisted; the idle to be spurred; the transgressors to be admonished or corrected; with the goers and comers to observe;—with all these things to be done, no considerable progress can be made, if one part of the wheel is not coming up to the work, while another is going down. And if order do not pervade the school, as a whole, and in all its parts, all is lost; and this is a very difficult thing;—for it seems as though the school were only a point, rescued out of a chaos that still encompasses it, and is ready, on the first opportunity, to break in and reoccupy its ancient possession. As it is utterly impracticable for any committee to prepare a code of regulations coextensive with all the details, which belong to the management of a school, it must be left with the teacher; and hence the necessity of skill in this item of the long list of his qualifications.

The government and discipline of a school demands qualities still more rare, because the consequences of error, in these, are still more disastrous. What caution, wisdom, uprightness, and sometimes, even intrepidity, are necessary in the administration of punishment. After all other means have been tried, and tried in vain, the chastisement of pupils found to be otherwise incorrigible, is still upheld by law, and sanctioned by public opinion. But it is the last resort, the ultimate resource, acknowledged, on all hands, to be a relic of barbarism, and yet authorized, because the community, although they feel it to be a great evil, have not yet devised and applied an antidote. Through an ignorance of the laws of health, a parent may so corrupt the constitution of his child, as to render poison a necessary medicine; and through an ignorance of the laws of mind, he may do the same thing in regard to punishment. When the arts of health and of education are understood, neither poison nor punishment will need to be used, unless in most extraordinary cases. The discipline of former times was inexorably stern and severe, and even if it were wished, it is impossible now to return to it. The question is, what can be substituted, which, without its severity, shall have its efficiency. . . .

4th. GOOD BEHAVIOR.—In two words, the statute opens, to all teachers, an extensive field of duty, by ordaining that all the youth in the schools shall be taught *"good behavior."* The framers of the law were aware, how rapidly good or bad manners mature into good or bad morals; they saw that good manners have not only the negative virtue of restraining from vice, but the positive one of leading, by imperceptible gradations, towards the practice of almost all the social virtues. The effects of civility or discourtesy, of gentlemanly or ungentlemanly deportment, are not periodical or occasional, merely, but of constant recurrence; and all the members of society have a direct interest in the manners of each of its individuals; because each one is a radiating point,—the centre of a circle, which he fills with pleasure or annoyance, not only for those who voluntarily enter it, but for those also, who, in the promiscuous movements of society, are caught within its circumference. Good behavior includes the elements of that equity, benevolence, conscience, which, in their great combinations, the moralist treats of in his books of ethics, and the legislator enjoins in his codes of law. The school room and its play-ground, next to the family table, are the places, where the selfish propensities come into most direct collision with social duties. Here, then, a right direction should be given to the growing mind. The surrounding influences, which are incorporated into its new thoughts and feelings, and make part of their substance, are too minute and subtile to be received in masses, like nourishment; they are rather imbibed into the system, unconsciously, by every act of respiration, and are constantly insinuating themselves into it, through all the avenues of the senses. If, then, the manners of the teacher are to be imitated by his pupils—if he is the glass, at which they "do dress themselves," how strong is the necessity, that he should understand those nameless and innumerable practices, in regard to deportment, dress, conversation, and all personal habits, that constitute the difference between a gentleman and a clown. We can bear some oddity, or eccentricity in a friend whom we admire for his talents, or revere for his virtues; but it becomes quite a different thing, when the oddity, or the eccentricity, is to be a pattern or model, from which fifty or a hundred children are to form their manners. It was well remarked, by the ablest British traveller who has ever visited this country, that amongst us, "every male above twenty-one years of age, claims to be a sovereign. He is, therefore, *bound to be a gentleman.*"

5th. Morals.—On the indispensable, all-controlling requisite of moral character, I have but a single suggestion to

LIVINGSTONE COLLEGE LIBRARY
SALISBURY. N. C.

make, in addition to those admirable views on this subject, which are scattered up and down through the committees' reports. This suggestion relates to the responsibility resting on those individuals, who give letters of recommendation, or certificates of character, to candidates for schools. . . . In the contemplation of the law, the school committee are sentinels stationed at the door of every schoolhouse in the State, to see that no teacher ever crosses its threshold, who is not clothed, from the crown of his head to the sole of his foot, in garments of virtue; and they are the enemies of the human race,—not of contemporaries only, but of posterity, —who, from any private or sinister motive, strive to put these sentinels to sleep, in order that one, who is profane, or intemperate, or addicted to low associations, or branded with the stigma of any vice, may elude the vigilance of the watchmen, and be installed over the pure minds of the young, as their guide and exemplar. If none but teachers of pure tastes, of good manners, of exemplary morals, had ever gained admission into our schools, neither the school rooms, nor their appurtenances would have been polluted, as some of them now are, with such ribald inscriptions, and with the carvings of such obscene emblems, as would make a heathen blush. Every person, therefore, who endorses another's character, as one befitting a school teacher, stands before the public as his moral bondsman and sponsor, and should be held to a rigid accountability.

Fifth Annual Report (1841)

Although the Fifth Report *again deals with schoolhouses, the qualifications of teachers, and the threat of religious dissension in the schools, its main body is given over to a masterful piece of salesmanship. Mann had questioned a number of Massachusetts businessmen concerning the over-all political and economic effects of common schooling. (For example, "Finally, in regard to those who possess the largest shares in the stock of worldly goods, could there, in your opinion, be any police so vigilant and effective, for the protection of all the rights of person, property and character, as such a sound and comprehensive education and training, as our system of Common Schools could be made to impart; and would not the payment of a sufficient tax to make such education and training universal, be the cheapest means of self-protection and insurance?") Basing his argument on the most favorable of the responses (to questions that were not entirely unloaded in the first place) he contended that businessmen should support public education on the most elementary grounds of self-interest, if no other. The* Fifth Report *was widely circulated and undoubtedly accomplished much in mobilizing business interest in the public schools.*

Sixth Annual Report (1842)

The Sixth Report *is a plea for health and physical education. Nowhere else in Mann's writings is the influence of phrenology in general and George Combe in particular so completely manifest. As is frequently the case with Mann's scientific commentaries, fact is liberally interspersed with fiction. Nonetheless, the over-all effect of the report was certainly beneficial at a time when even the most elementary rules of health were unknown to most people.*

Seventh Annual Report (1843)

Mann went abroad in the spring of 1843 for a school inspection tour which took him through England, Ireland, Scotland, Germany, Holland, Belgium, and France. His observations and comments on the institutions he visted form the body of the Seventh Report, *a fascinating venture into the realm of comparative education. Mann's glowing comments on Pestalozzian methods in the Prussian schools evoked sharp criticism from an ad hoc association of Boston schoolmasters, and throughout 1844 he was involved in a running battle of rejoinders and rejoinders to rejoinders. While the report is meritorious in its own right, it is principally on account of this exchange that it is the best known of the twelve. The following excerpt on student–teacher relationships in the Prussian schools provides insight into the kind of comment which irked the masters.*

The third circumstance I mentioned above was the beautiful relation of harmony and affection which subsisted between teacher and pupils. I cannot say that the extraordinary fact I have mentioned was not the result of chance or accident. Of the probability of that, others must judge. I can only say that, during all the time mentioned, I never saw a blow struck, I never heard a sharp rebuke given, I never saw a child in tears, nor arraigned at the teacher's bar for any alleged misconduct. On the contrary, the relation seemed to be one of duty first, and then affection, on the part of the teacher,—of affection first, and then duty, on the part of the scholar. The teacher's manner was better than parental, for it had a parent's tenderness and vigilance, without the foolish doatings or indulgences to which parental affection is prone. I heard no child ridiculed, sneered at, or scolded, for making a mistake. On the contrary, whenever a mistake was made, or there was a want of promptness in giving a reply, the expression of the teacher was that of grief and disappointment, as though there had been a failure, not merely to answer the question of a master, but to comply with the expectations of a friend. No child was disconcerted, disabled, or bereft of his senses, through fear. Nay, generally, at the ends of the answers, the teacher's practice is to encourage him with the exclamation, 'good,' 'right,' 'wholly right,' &c., or to check him, with his slowly and painfully articulated 'no;' and this is done with a tone of voice that marks every degree of *plus* and *minus* in the scale of approbation or regret. When a difficult question has been put to a young child, which tasks all his energies, the teacher approaches him with a mingled look of concern and encouragement; he stands before him, the light and shade of hope and fear alternately crossing his contenance; he lifts his arms and turns his body,—as a bowler who has given a wrong direction to his bowl will writhe his person to bring the ball back upon its track;—and finally, if the little wrestler with difficulty triumphs, the teacher felicitates him upon his success, perhaps seizes and shakes him by the hand, in token of congratulation; and, when the difficulty has been really formidable, and the effort triumphant, I have seen the teacher catch up the child in his arms and embrace him, as though he were not able to contain his joy.

At another time, I have seen a teacher actually clap his hands with delight at a bright reply; and all this has been done so naturally and so unaffectedly as to excite no other feeling in the residue of the children than a desire, by the same means, to win the same caresses. What person worthy of being called by the name, or of sustaining the sacred relation of a parent, would not give anything, bear anything, sacrifice anything, to have his children, during eight or ten years of the period of their childhood, surrounded by circumstances, and breathed upon by sweet and humanizing influences, like these!

I mean no disparagement of our own teachers by the remark I am about to make. As a general fact, these teachers are as good as public opinion has demanded; as good as the public sentiment has been disposed to appreciate; as good as public liberality has been ready to reward; as good as the preliminary measures taken to qualify them would authorize us to expect. But it was impossible to put down the questionings of my own mind—whether a visiter could spend six weeks in our own schools without ever hearing an angry word spoken, or seeing a blow struck, or witnessing the flow of tears.

Eighth Annual Report (1844)

The Eighth Report *has no central theme, unless it be the multifarious problems which beset a growing public school system. There are capsule discussions of private schools, school appropriations, disciplinary problems, the employment of female teachers, and the beneficial effects of teacher institutes. Probably the most novel aspect of the report is an extended commentary on the values of vocal music in the schools. One wonders again at the quaintness of remarks about how music curbs the passions. Yet is it surprising to find a moralist seeking moral values in everything he favors?*

Ninth Annual Report (1845)

The compensation, social status, and education of teachers are again discussed in the Ninth Report, *as is the more general progress of the Massachusetts schools. The central theme, however, is the primacy of moral over intellectual education; and a long section on the pedagogy of moral education once more draws heavily on Combe and Pestalozzi. The following extract discusses the problem of discipline in the schools of a free people.*

One of the highest and most valuable objects, to which the influences of a school can be made conducive, consists in training our children to self-government. The doctrine of No-government, even if all forms of violence did not meet, the first day, to celebrate its introduction by a jubilee, would forfeit all the power that originates in concert and union. So tremendous, too, are the evils of anarchy and lawlessness, that a government by mere force, however arbitrary and cruel, has been held preferable to no-government. But self-government, self-control, a voluntary compliance with the laws of reason and duty, have been justly considered as the highest point of excellence attainable by a human being. No one, however, can consciously obey the laws of reason and duty, until he understands them. Hence the preliminary necessity of their being clearly explained, of their being made to stand out, broad, lofty, and as conspicuous as a mountain against a clear sky. There may be blind obedience without a knowledge of the law, but only of the will of the lawgiver; but the first step towards rational obedience is a knowledge of the rule to be obeyed, and of the reasons on which it is founded.

The above doctrine acquires extraordinary force, in view

of our political institutions,—founded, as they are, upon
the great idea of the capacity of man for self-government,—
an idea so long denounced by the state as treasonable, and
by the church as heretical. In order that men may be prepared for self-government, their apprenticeship must commence in childhood. The great moral attribute of self-government cannot be born and matured in a day; and if
school children are not trained to it, we only prepare ourselves for disappointment, if we expect it from grown men.
Every body acknowledges the justness of the declaration,
that a foreign people, born and bred and dwarfed under the
despotisms of the Old World, cannot be transformed into
the full stature of American citizens, merely by a voyage
across the Atlantic, or by subscribing the oath of naturaliza-
tion. If they retain the servility in which they have been
trained, some self-appointed lord or priest, on this side of
the water, will succeed to the authority of the master, they
have left behind them. If, one the other hand, they identify
liberty with an absence from restraint, and an immunity
from punishment, then they are liable to become intoxicated
and delirious with the highly stimulating properties of the
air of freedom; and thus, in either case, they remain un-
fitted, until they have become morally acclimated to our
institutions, to exercise the rights of a freeman. But can it
make any substantial difference, whether a man is suddenly
translated into all the independence and prerogatives of an
American citizen, from the bondage of an Irish lord or an
English manufacturer, or from the equally rigorous bondage
of a parent, guardian or school teacher? He who has been a
serf until the day before he is twenty-one years of age, cannot be an independent citizen the day after; and it makes
no difference whether he has been a serf in Austria or in
America. As the fitting apprenticeship for despotism consists in being trained to despotism, so the fitting apprenticeship for self-government consists in being trained to self-
government; and liberty and self-imposed law are as appropriate a preparation for the subjects of an arbitrary power,
as the law of force and authority is for developing and maturing those sentiments of self-respect, of honor and of
dignity, which belong to a truly republican citizen. Were we
hereafter to govern irresponsibly, then our being forced

to yield implicit obedience to an irresponsible governor would prepare us to play the tyrant in our turn; but if we are to govern by virtue of a law which embraces all, which overlies all, which includes the governor as well as the governed, then lessons of obedience should be inculcated upon childhood, in reference to that sacred law. If there are no two things wider asunder than freedom and slavery, then must the course of training which fits children for these two opposite conditions of life be as diverse as the points to which they lead. Now, for the high purpose of training an American child to become an American citizen,—a constituent part of a self-governing people,—is it not obvious that, in all cases, the law by which he is to be bound should be made intelligible to him; and, as soon as his capacity will permit, that the reasons on which it is founded, should be made as intelligible as the law itself?

Tenth Annual Report (1846)

The Tenth Report *is a general discourse on the Massachusetts schools. While much of it is devoted to a lengthy exposition of the state education code, Mann includes an illuminating discussion of the general principles governing the public school system. Most of this discussion is included in the following excerpt.*

As an innovation upon all preëxisting policy and usages, the establishment of Free Schools was the boldest ever promulgated, since the commencement of the Christian era. As a theory, it could have been refuted and silenced by a more formidable array of argument and experience than was ever marshalled against any other opinion of human origin. But time has ratified its soundness. Two centuries now proclaim it to be as wise as it was courageous, as beneficent as it was disinterested. It was one of those grand mental and moral experiments whose effects cannot be determined in a single generation. But now, according to the manner in which human life is computed, we are the sixth generation from its founders, and have we not reason to be grateful both to God and man for its unnumbered blessings? The sincerity of our gratitude must be tested by our efforts to perpetuate and improve what they established. The gratitude of the lips only is an unholy offering.

In surveying our vast country,—the rich savannahs of the South and the almost interminable prairies of the West,— that great valley, where, if all the nations of Europe were set down together, they could find ample subsistence,—the ejaculation involuntarily bursts forth, "WHY WERE THEY NOT COLONIZED BY MEN LIKE THE PILGRIM FATHERS!"—and as we reflect, how different would have been the fortunes of this nation, had those States,—already so numerous, and still extending, circle beyond circle,—been founded by men of high, heroic, Puritan mould;—how different in the eye of a righteous Heaven, how different in the estimation of the wise and good of all contemporary nations, how different in the fortunes of that vast procession of the generations which are yet to rise up over all those wide expanses, and to follow each other to the end of time;—as we reflect upon these things, it seems almost pious to repine at the ways of Providence; resignation becomes laborious, and we are forced to choke down our murmurings at the will of Heaven! Is it the solution of this deep mystery, that our ancestors did as much in their time, as it is ever given to one generation of men to accomplish, and have left to us and to our descendants the completion of the glorious work they began?

The alleged ground upon which the founders of our Free School system proceeded, when adopting it, did not embrace the whole argument by which it may be defended. Their insight was better than their reason. They assumed a ground, indeed, satisfactory and convincing to Protestants; but, at that time, only a small portion of Christendom was Protestant, and even now only a minority of it is so. The very ground on which our Free Schools were founded, therefore, if it were the only one, would be a reason with half of Christendom, at the present time, for their immediate abolition.

In later times, and since the achievement of American Independence, the universal and ever-repeated argument in favor of Free Schools has been, that the general intelligence which they are capable of diffusing, and which can be imparted by no other human instrumentality, is indispensable to the continuance of a republican government. This argument, it is obvious, assumes, as a postulatum, the superiority of a republican over all other forms of government; and, as a people, we religiously believe in the soundness, both of the assumption and of the argument founded upon it. But if this be all, then a sincere monarchist, a defender of arbitrary power, or a believer in the divine right of kings, would oppose Free Schools, for the identical reasons we offer in their behalf. A perfect demonstration of our doctrine,—that Free Schools are the only basis of republican institutions,— would be the perfection of reasoning to his mind, that they should be immediately exterminated.

Admitting, nay claiming for ourselves, the substantial justness and soundness of the general grounds on which our system was originally established and has since been maintained; yet it is most obvious that, unless some broader and more comprehensive principle can be found, the system of Free Schools will be repudiated by whole nations as impolitic and dangerous; and, even among ourselves, all who deny our premises will, of course, set at nought the conclusions to which they lead.

Again; the expediency of Free Schools is sometimes advocated on grounds of Political Economy. An educated people is a more industrious and productive people. Knowledge and abundance sustain to each other the relation of cause and effect. Intelligence is a primary ingredient in the Wealth of Nations. Where this does not stand at the head of the inventory, the items in a nation's valuation will be few, and the sum at the foot of the column insignificant.

The moralist, too, takes up the argument of the economist. He demonstrates that vice and crime are not only prodigals and spendthrifts of their own, but defrauders and plunderers of the means of others; that they would seize upon all the gains of honest industry, and exhaust the bounties of Heaven itself, without satiating their rapacity for new means of indulgence; and that often, in the history of the world, whole generations might have been trained to industry and virtue by the wealth which one enemy to his race has destroyed.

And yet, notwithstanding these views have been presented a thousand times, with irrefutable logic, and with a divine eloquence of truth which it would seem that nothing but combined stolidity and depravity could resist, there is not at the present time, with the exception of New England and a few small localities elsewhere, a State or a community in Christendom, which maintains a system of Free Schools for the education of its children. Even in the State of New York, with all its noble endowments, the Schools are not Free.

I believe that this amazing dereliction from duty, especially in our own country, originates more in the false notions which men entertain *respecting the nature of their right to property*, than in any thing else. In the district school meeting, in the town meeting, in legislative halls, every where, the advocates for a more generous education could carry their respective audiences with them in behalf of increased privileges for our children, were it not instinctively foreseen that increased privileges must be followed by increased taxation. Against this obstacle argument falls dead. The rich man, who has no children, declares it to be an invasion of his rights of property to exact a contribution from him to educate the children of his neighbor. The man who has reared and educated a family of children denounces it as a double tax, when he is called upon to assist in educating the children of others also; or, if he has reared his own children, without educating them, he thinks it peculiarly oppressive to be obliged to do for others, what he refrained from doing even for himself. Another, having children, but disdaining to educate them with the common mass, withdraws them from the Public School, puts them under what he calls "selecter influences," and then thinks it a grievance to be obliged to support a school which he contemns. Or if these different parties so far yield to the force of traditionary sentiment and usage, and to the public opinion around them, as to consent to do something for the cause, they soon reach the limit of expense where their admitted obligation, or their alleged charity, terminates.

It seems not irrelevant, therefore, in this connection, to

inquire into the nature of a man's right to the property he possesses, and to satisfy ourselves respecting the question, whether any man has such an indefeasible title to his estates, or such an absolute ownership of them, as renders it unjust in the government to assess upon him his share of the expenses of educating the children of the community, up to such a point as the nature of the institutions under which he lives, and the well-being of society require.

I believe in the existence of a great, immutable principle of natural law, or natural ethics,—a principle antecedent to all human institutions and incapable of being abrogated by any ordinances of man,—a principle of divine origin, clearly legible in the ways of Providence as those ways are manifested in the order of nature and in the history of the race, —which proves the *absolute right* of every human being that comes into the world to an education; and which, of course, proves the correlative duty of every government to see that the means of that education are provided for all.

In regard to the application of this principle of natural law,—that is, in regard to the extent of the education to be provided for all, at the public expense,—some differences of opinion may fairly exist, under different political organizations; but under a republican government, it seems clear that the minimum of this education can never be less than such as is sufficient to qualify each citizen for the civil and social duties he will be called to discharge;—such an education as teaches the individual the great laws of bodily health; as qualifies for the fulfilment of parental duties; as is indispensable for the civil functions of a witness or a juror; as is necessary for the voter in municipal affairs; and finally, for the faithful and conscientious discharge of all those duties which devolve upon the inheritor of a portion of the sovereignty of this great republic.

The will of God, as conspicuously manifested in the order of nature, and in the relations which he has established among men, places the *right* of every child that is born into the world to such a degree of education as will enable him, and, as far as possible, will predispose him, to perform all domestic, social, civil and moral duties, upon the same clear ground of natural law and equity, as it places a child's *right,* upon his first coming into the world, to distend his lungs with a portion of the common air, or to open his eyes to the common light, or to receive that shelter, protection and nourishment which are necessary to the continuance of his bodily existence. And so far is it from being a wrong or a hardship, to demand of the possessors of property their respective shares for the prosecution of this divinely-ordained work, that they themselves are guilty of the most far-reaching injustice, who seek to resist or to evade the contribution. The complainers are the wrong-doers. The cry, "Stop thief," comes from the thief himself.

To any one who looks beyond the mere surface of things, it is obvious, that the primary and natural elements or ingredients of all property consist in the riches of the soil, in the treasures of the sea, in the light and warmth of the sun, in the fertilizing clouds and streams and dews, in the winds, and in the chemical and vegetative agencies of nature. In the majority of cases, all that we call *property,* all that makes up the valuation or inventory of a nation's capital, was prepared at the creation, and was laid up of old in the capacious store-houses of nature. For every unit that a man earns by his own toil or skill, he receives hundreds and thousands, without cost and without recompense, from the All-bountiful Giver. A proud mortal, standing in the midst of his luxuriant wheat-fields or cotton-plantations, may arrogantly call them his own; yet what barren wastes would they be, did not heaven send down upon them its dews and its rains, its warmth and its light; and sustain, for their growth and ripening, the grateful vicissitude of the seasons? It is said that from eighty to ninety per cent of the very substance of some of the great staples of agriculture are not taken from the earth but are absorbed from the air; so that these productions may more properly be called fruits of the atmosphere than of the soil. Who prepares this elemental wealth; who scatters it, like a sower, through all the regions of the atmosphere, and sends the richly-freighted winds, as His messengers, to bear to each leaf in the forest and to each blade in the cultivated field, the nourishment which their infinitely-varied needs demand? Aided by machinery, a single manufacturer performs the labor of hundreds of men. Yet what could he accomplish without the weight of the waters which God causes ceaselessly to flow; or without those gigantic forces which He has given to steam? And how would the commerce of the world be carried on, were it not for those great laws of nature,—of electricity, of condensation and of rarefaction,—that give birth to the winds, which, in conformity to the will of Heaven, and not in obedience to any power of man, forever traverse the earth, and offer themselves as an unchartered medium for interchanging the products of all the zones? These few references show how vast a proportion of all the wealth which men presumptuously call their own, because they claim to have earned it, is poured into their lap, unasked and unthanked for, by the Being, so infinitely gracious in his physical, as well as in his moral bestowments.

But for whose subsistence and benefit, were these exhaustless treasuries of wealth created? Surely not for any one man, nor for any one generation; but for the subsistence and benefit of the whole race, from the beginning to the end of time. They were not created for Adam alone, nor for Noah alone, nor for the first discoverers or colonists who may have found or have peopled any part of the earth's ample domain. No! They were created for the race, collectively, but to be possessed and enjoyed in succession, as the generations, one after another, should come into existence;—equal rights, with a successive enjoyment of them! If we consider the earth and the fulness thereof, as one great habitation or domain, then each generation, subject to certain modifications for the encouragement of industry and frugality,—which modifications it is not necessary here to specify,—has only a life lease in them. There are certain reasonable regulations in regard to the out-going and the incoming tenants, —regulations which allow to the out-going generations a brief control over their property after they are called upon to leave it, and which also allow the incoming generations to anticipate a little their full right of possession. But, subject to these regulations, nature ordains a perpetual entail and transfer, from one generation to another, of all property in the great, substantive, enduring elements of wealth;—in the soil; in metals and minerals; in precious stones, and in more precious coal and iron and granite; in the waters and winds and sun;—and no one man, nor any one generation of men has any such title to, or ownership in, these ingredients and substantials of all wealth, that his right is invaded when a portion of them is taken for the benefit of posterity.

This great principle of natural law may be illustrated by a reference to some of the unstable elements, in regard to which the *property* of each individual is strongly qualified in relation to his contemporaries, even while he has the acknowledged right of *possession*. Take the streams of water, or the wind, for example. A stream, as it descends from its sources to its mouth, is successively the property of all those through whose land it passes. My neighbor who lives above me owned it yesterday, while it was passing through his lands; I own it today, while it is descending through mine, and the contiguous proprietor below will own it to-morrow, while it is flowing through his, as it passes onward to the next. But the rights of the successive owners are not absolute and unqualified. They are limited by the rights of those who are entitled to the subsequent possession and use. While a stream is passing through my lands, I may not corrupt it, so that it shall be offensive or valueless to the adjoining proprietor below. I may not stop it in its downward course, nor divert it into any other direction so that it shall leave his channel dry. I may lawfully use it for various purposes,—for agriculture, as in irrigating lands or watering cattle; for manufactures, as in turning wheels, &c.,—but in all my uses of it, I must pay regard to the rights of my neighbors lower down. So no two proprietors, nor any half-dozen proprietors, by conspiring together, can deprive an owner who lives below them all, of the ultimate right which he has to the use of the stream in its descending course. We see here, therefore, that a man has certain qualified rights,—rights of which he cannot be divested without his own consent,—in a stream of water, before it reaches the limits of his own estate;—at which latter point, he may, somewhat more emphatically, call it his own. And in this sense, a man who lives at the outlet of a river, on the margin of the ocean, has certain incipient rights in the fountains that well up from the earth, at the distance of thousands of miles.

So it is with the ever-moving winds. No man has a *permanent* interest in the breezes that blow by him, and bring healing and refreshment on their wings. Each man has a temporary interest in them. From whatever quarter of the compass they may come, I have a right to use them as they are passing by me; yet that use must always be regulated by the rights of those other participants and co-owners whom they are moving forward to bless. It is not lawful, therefore, for me to corrupt them, to load them with noxious gases or vapors, by which they will prove valueless or detrimental to him, whoever he may be, towards whom they are moving.

In one respect, indeed, the winds illustrate our relative rights and duties, even better than the streams. In the latter case, the rights are not only successive, but always in the same order of priority,—those of the owner above necessarily preceding those of the owner below; and this order is unchangeable, except by changing the ownership of the land itself to which the rights are appurtenant. But in the case of the winds which blow from every quarter of the heavens, I may have the prior right to-day, and with a change in their direction, my neighbor may have it to-morrow. If, therefore, to-day, when the wind is going from me to him, I should usurp the right to use it to his detriment; to-morrow, when it is coming from him to me, he may inflict retributive usurpation upon me.

The light of the sun, too, is subject to the same benign and equitable regulations. As this ethereal element passes by me, I have a right to bask in its genial beams, or to employ its quickening powers. But I have no right, even on my own land, to build up a wall, mountain-high, that shall eclipse the sun to my neighbor's eyes.

Now all these great principles of natural law, which define and limit the rights of neighbors and contemporaries, are incorporated into, and constitute a part of, the civil law of every civilized people; and they are obvious and simple illustrations of the great proprietary laws by which individuals and generations hold their rights in the solid substance of the globe, in the elements that move over its surface, and in the chemical and vital powers with which it is so marvellously endued. As successive owners on a river's banks have equal rights to the waters that flow through their respective domains, subject only to the modification that the proprietors nearer the stream's source must have precedence in the enjoyment of their rights over those lower down; so the rights of all the generations of mankind to the earth itself, to the streams that fertilize it, to the winds that purify it, to the vital principles that animate it, and to the reviving light, are common rights, though subject to similar modifications in regard to preceding and succeeding generations. They did not belong to our ancestors in perpetuity; they do not belong to us in perpetuity; and the right of the next generation in them will be limited and defeasible like ours. As we hold them subject to their claims, so will they hold them subject to the claims of their immediate successors, and so on to the end of time. And the savage tribes that roam about the head-springs of the Mississippi have as good a right to ordain what use shall be made of its copious waters, when, in their grand descent across a continent, they shall reach the shores of arts and civilization, as any of our predecessors had, or as we ourselves have, to say what shall be done, *in perpetuity,* with the soil, the waters, the winds, the light, and the invisible agencies of nature, which must be allowed, on all hands, to constitute the indispensable elements of wealth.

Is not the inference irresistible, then, that no man, by whatever means he may have come into possession of his property, has any natural right, any more than he has a moral one, to hold it, or to dispose of it, irrespective of the needs and claims of those, who, in the august procession of the generations, are to be his successors on the stage of existence? Holding his rights subject to their rights, he is bound not to impair the value of their inheritance, either by commission or by omission.

Generation after generation proceeds from the creative energy of God. Each one stops for a brief period upon the earth, resting, as it were, only for a night,—like migratory birds upon their passage,—and then leaving it forever to others whose existence is as transitory as its own; and the migratory flocks of water-fowl which sweep across our latitudes in their passage to another clime, have as good a right to make a perpetual appropriation, to their own use, of the lands over which they fly, as any one generation has to arrogate perpetual dominion and sovereignty for its own purposes over that portion of the earth which it is its fortune to occupy during the brief period of its temporal existence.

Another consideration, bearing upon this arrogant doctrine of absolute ownership or sovereignty, has hardly less force than the one just expounded. We have seen how insignificant a portion of any man's possessions he can claim, in any proper and just sense, *to have earned;* and that, in regard to all the residue, he is only taking his turn in the use of a bounty bestowed, in common, by the Giver of all, upon his ancestors, himself, and his posterity,—a line of indefinite length, in which he is but a point. But this is not the only deduction to be made from his assumed rights. The *present* wealth of the world has an additional element in it. Much of all that is capable of being earned by man, has been earned by our predecessors, and has come down to us in a solid and enduring form. We have not built all the houses in which we live; nor all the roads on which we travel; nor all the ships in which we carry on our commerce with the world. We have not reclaimed from the wilderness all the fields whose harvests we now reap; and if we had no precious metals, or stones, or pearls, but such as we ourselves had dug from the mines, or brought up from the bottom of the ocean, our coffers and our caskets would be empty indeed. But even if this were not so, whence came all the arts and sciences, the discoveries and the inventions, without which, and without a common right to which, the valuation of the property of a whole nation would scarcely equal the inventory of a single man,—without which, indeed, we should now be in a state of barbarism. Whence came a knowledge of agriculture, without which we should have so little to reap; or a knowledge of astronomy, without which we could not traverse the oceans; or a knowledge of chemistry and mechanical philosophy without which the arts and trades could not exist? Most of all this was found out by those who have gone before us, and some of it has come down to us from a remote antiquity. Surely all these boons and blessings belong as much to posterity as to ourselves. They have not descended to us to be arrested and consumed here, or to be sequestrated from the ages to come. Cato and Archimedes and Kepler and Newton and Franklin and Arkwright and Fulton, and all the bright host of benefactors to science and art, did not make, or bequeath their discoveries or inventions to benefit any one generation, but to increase the common enjoyments of mankind to the end of time. So of all the great law-givers and moralists who have improved the civil institutions of the State, who have made it dangerous to be wicked, or,—far better than this,—have made it hateful to be so. Resources developed, property acquired, after all these ages of preparation, after all these facilities and securities, accrue not to the benefit of the possessor only, but to that of the next and of all succeeding generations.

Surely, these considerations limit still more extensively that absolutism of ownership which is so often claimed by the possessors of wealth.

But sometimes, the rich farmer, the opulent manufacturer, or the capitalist, when sorely pressed with his legal and moral obligation, to contribute a portion of his means for the education of the young, replies,—either in form or in spirit;—"My lands, my machinery, my gold and my silver, are mine; may not I do what I will with my own?" There is one supposable case, and only one, where this argument would have plausibility. If it were made by an isolated, solitary being,—a being having no relations to a community around him, having no ancestors to whom he had been indebted for ninety-nine parts in every hundred of all he possesses, and expecting to leave no posterity after him,—it might not be easy to answer it. If there were but one family in this western hemisphere, and one only in the eastern hemisphere, and these two families bore no civil and social relations to each other, and were to be the first and last of the whole race, it might be difficult, except on very high and almost transcendental grounds, for either one of them to show good cause why the other should contribute to help to educate children not his own. And perhaps the force of such an appeal would be still further diminished, if the nearest neighbor of a single family upon our planet were as far from the earth as Uranus or Sirius. In self-defence, or in selfishness, one might say to the other, "What are your fortunes to me? You can neither benefit nor molest me. Let us each keep to our own side of the planetary spaces." But is this the relation which any man amongst us sustains to his fellows? In the midst of a populous community to which

he is bound by innumerable ties, having had his own fortune and condition almost predetermined and foreordained
by his predecessors, and being about to exert upon his successors as commanding an influence as has been exerted
upon himself, the objector can no longer shrink into his
individuality, and disclaim connection and relationship with
the world. He cannot deny that there are thousands around
him on whom he acts, and who are continually reäcting
upon him. The earth is much too small, or the race is far
too numerous, to allow us to be hermits, and therefore we
cannot adopt either the philosophy or the morals of hermits.
All have derived benefits from their ancestors, and all are
bound, as by an oath, to transmit those benefits, even in an
improved condition, to posterity. We may as well attempt
to escape from our own personal identity, as to shake off
the three-fold relation which we bear to others,—the relation of an associate with our contemporaries; of a bene-
ficiary of our ancestors; of a guardian to those who, in the
sublime order of Providence, are to follow us. Out of these
relations, manifest duties are evolved. The society of which
we necessarily constitute a part, must be preserved; and, in
order to preserve it, we must not look merely to what one
individual or family needs, but to what the whole community needs; not merely to what one generation needs, but to
the wants of a succession of generations. To draw conclusions without considering these facts, is to leave out the
most important part of the premises.

A powerfully corroborating fact remains untouched.
Though the earth and the beneficent capabilities with
which it is endued, belong in common to the race; yet we
find that previous and present possessors have laid their
hands upon the whole of it;—have left no part of it un-
claimed and unappropriated. They have circumnavigated
the globe; they have drawn lines across every habitable
portion of it, and have partitioned amongst themselves, not
only its whole area, or superficial contents, but have claimed
it down to the centre, and up to the concave;—a great in-
verted pyramid for each proprietor,—so that not an un-
claimed rood is left, either in the caverns below, or in the
aërial spaces above, where a new adventurer upon existence
can take unresisted possession. They have entered into a

solemn compact with each other for mutual protection of
their respective parts. They have created legislators and
judges and executive officers, who denounce and inflict penalties even to the taking of life; and they have organized
armed bands to repel aggression upon their claims. Indeed,
so grasping and rapacious have mankind been, in this particular, that they have taken more than they could use, more
than they could perambulate and survey, more than they
could see from the top of the mast-head, or from the highest
peak of the mountain. There was some limit to their physical power of taking possession, but none to the exorbitancy
of their desires. Like robbers, who divide their spoils, before
they know whether they shall find a victim, men have
claimed a continent while still doubtful of its existence, and
spread out their title from ocean to ocean, before their most
adventurous pioneers had ever seen a shore of the realms
they coveted. The whole planet, then, having been appropriated; there being no waste or open lands, from which the
new generations may be supplied as they come into existence, have not those generations the strongest conceivable
claim upon the present occupants, for that which is indispensable to their well-being? They have more than a pre-
ëmptive, they have a possessory right to some portion of the
issues and profits of that, all of which has been taken up
and appropriated. A denial of this right by the present
possessors, is a breach of trust,—a fraudulent misuse of
power given, and of confidence reposed. On mere principles
of political economy, it is folly; on the broader principles of
duty and morality, it is embezzlement.

It is not at all in contravention of this view of the subject, that the adult portion of society does take, and must
take, upon itself, the control and management of all existing
property, until the rising generation has arrived at the age
of majority. Nay, one of the objects of their so doing is to
preserve the rights of the generation which is still in its
minority. Society, to this extent, is only a trustee managing
an estate for the benefit of a part-owner, or of one who has
a reversionary interest in it. This civil regulation, therefore,
made necessary even for the benefit of both present and
future possessors, is only in furtherance of the great law
under consideration.

THE EDUCATION OF FREE MEN

Coincident, too, with this great law, but in no manner superseding or invalidating it, is that wonderful provision which the Creator has made for the care of offspring, in the affection of their parents. Heaven did not rely merely upon our perceptions of duty towards our children, and our fidelity in its performance. A powerful, all-mastering instinct of love was therefore implanted in the parental, and especially in the maternal breast, to anticipate the idea of duty, and to make duty delightful. Yet the great doctrine, founded upon the will of God, as made known to us in the natural order and relation of things, would still remain the same, though all that beautiful portion of our moral being, whence parental affection springs, were a void and a nonentity. Emphatically would the obligations of society remain the same for all those children who have been bereaved of parents; or who, worse than bereavement, have only monster-parents of intemperance, or cupidity, or of any other of those forms of vice, that seem to suspend or to obliterate the law of love in the parental breast. For these, society is doubly bound to be a parent, and to exercise all that rational care and providence which a wise father would exercise for his own children.

If the previous argument began with sound premises and has been logically conducted, then it has established this position;—that a vast portion of the present wealth of the world either consists in, or has been immediately derived from, those great natural substances and powers of the earth, which were bestowed by the Creator, alike on all mankind, or from the discoveries, inventions, labors and improvements of our ancestors, which were alike designed for the common benefit of all their descendants. The question now arises, *at what time,* is this wealth to be transferred from a preceding to a succeeding generation? At what point, are the latter to take possession of, or to derive benefit from it, or at what time, are the former to surrender it in their behalf? Is each existing generation, and each individual of an existing generation, to hold fast to his possessions until death relaxes his grasp; or is something of the right to be acknowledged, and something of the benefit to be yielded, beforehand? It seems too obvious for argument, that the latter is the only alternative. If the incoming generation have no rights until the outgoing generation have actually retired, then is every individual that enters the world liable to perish on the day he is born. According to the very constitution of things, each individual must obtain sustenance and succor, as soon as his eyes open to the light, or his lungs are inflated by the air. His wants cannot be delayed until he himself can supply them. If the demands of his nature are ever to be answered, they must be answered years before he can make any personal provision for them, either by the performance of labor, or by any exploits of skill. The infant must be fed, before he can earn his bread; he must be clothed before he can prepare garments; he must be protected from the elements before he can erect a dwelling; and it is just as clear that he must be instructed before he can engage a tutor. A course contrary to this, would be the destruction of the young, that we might withhold their rightful inheritance. Carried to its extreme, it would be the act of Herod, seeking, in a general massacre, the life of one who was supposed to endanger his power. Here, then, the claims of the succeeding generation, not only upon the affection and the care, but upon the *property* of the preceding one, attach. God having given to the second generation as full and complete a right to the incomes and profits of the world, as he has given to the first; and to the third generation as full and complete a right as he has given to the second, and so on while the world stands; it necessarily follows that children must come into a partial and qualified possession of these rights, by the paramount law of nature, as soon as they are born. No human enactments can abolish or countervail this paramount and supreme law; and all those positive, and often arbitrary enactments of the civil code, by which, for the encouragement of industry and frugality, the possessor of property is permitted to control it for a limited period after his decease, must be construed and executed in subservience to this sovereign and irrepealable ordinance of nature.

Nor is this transfer always, or even generally, to be made *in kind;* but according to the needs of the recipient. The recognition of this principle is universal. A guardian or trustee may possess lands, while the ward, or owner under the trust, may need money; or the former may have money, while the latter need raiment or shelter. The form of the estate must be changed, if need be, and adapted to the wants of the receiver.

The claim of a child, then, to a portion of preëxistent property begins with the first breath he draws. The new-born infant must have sustenance and shelter and care. If the natural parents are removed, or parental ability fails,—in a word, if parents either cannot or will not supply the infant's wants, then society at large,—the government,—having assumed to itself the ultimate control of all property,—is bound to step in and fill the parent's place. To deny this to any child would be equivalent to a sentence of death,—a capital execution of the innocent,—at which every soul shudders! It would be a more cruel form of infanticide than any which is practised in China or in Africa.

But to preserve the animal life of a child only, and there to stop, would be,—not the bestowment of a blessing or the performance of a duty,—but the infliction of a fearful curse. A child has interests far higher than those of mere physical existence. Better that the wants of the natural life should be disregarded, than that the higher interests of the character should be neglected. If a child has any claim to bread to keep him from perishing, he has a far higher claim to knowledge to preserve him from error and its fearful retinue of calamities. If a child has any claim to shelter to protect him from the destroying elements, he has a far higher claim to be rescued from the infamy and perdition of vice and crime.

All moralists agree, nay, all moralists maintain, that a man is as responsible for his omissions as for his commissions;—that he is as guilty of the wrong which he could have prevented, but did not, as for that which his own hand has perpetrated. They then, who knowingly withhold sustenance from a new-born child, and he dies, are guilty of infanticide. And, by the same reasoning, they who refuse to enlighten the intellect of the rising generation, are guilty of degrading the human race! They who refuse to train up children in the way they should go, are training up incendiaries and madmen to destroy property and life, and to invade and pollute the sanctuaries of society! In a word, if the mind is as real and substantive a part of human existence as the body, then mental attributes during the periods of childhood, demand provision at least as imperatively as bodily appetites. The time when these respective obligations attach, corresponds with the periods when the nurture, whether physical or mental, is needed. As the right of sustenance is of equal date with birth, so the right to intellectual and moral training begins, at least as early as when children are ordinarily sent to school. At that time, then, by the irrepealable law of nature, every child succeeds to so much more of the property of the community as is necessary for his education. He is to receive this, not in the form of lands, or of gold and silver, but in the form of knowledge and a training to good habits. This is one of the steps in the transfer of the property of the present to a succeeding generation. Human sagacity may be at fault in fixing the amount of property to be transferred, or the time when the transfer should be made, to a dollar or to an hour; but certainly, in a republican government, the obligation of the predecessors, and the right of the successors, extend to and embrace the means of such an amount of education as will prepare each individual to perform all the duties which devolve upon him as a man and a citizen. It may go further than this point; certainly, it cannot fall short of it.

Under our political organization, the places and the processes where this transfer is to be provided for, and its amount determined, are the district school meeting, the town meeting, legislative halls, and conventions for establishing or revising the fundamental laws of the State. If it be not done there, society is false to its high trusts; and any community, whether national or state, that ventures to organize a government, or to administer a government already organized, without making provision for the free education of all its children, dares the certain vengeance of Heaven; and, in the squalid forms of poverty and destitution, in the scourges of violence and misrule, in the heart-destroying corruptions of licentiousness and debauchery, and in political profligacy and legalized perfidy,—in all the blended and mutually aggravated crimes of civilization and of barbarism, will be sure to feel the terrible retributions of its delinquency.

I bring my argument on this point, then, to a close; and I present a test of its validity, which, as it seems to me, defies denial or evasion.

In obedience to the laws of God and to the laws of all civilized communities, society is bound to protect the natural life; and the natural life cannot be protected without the appropriation and use of a portion of the property which society possesses. We prohibit infanticide under penalty of death. We practise a refinement in this particular. The life of an infant is inviolable even before he is born; and he who feloniously takes it, even before birth, is as subject to the extreme penalty of the law, as though he had struck down manhood in its vigor, or taken away a mother by violence from the sanctuary of home, where she blesses her offspring. But why preserve the natural life of a child, why preserve unborn embryos of life, if we do not intend to watch over and to protect them, and to expand their subsequent existence into usefulness and happiness? As individuals, or as an organized community, we have no natural right; we can derive no authority or countenance from reason; we can cite no attribute or purpose of the divine nature, for giving birth to any human being, and then inflicting upon that being the curse of ignorance, of poverty and of vice, with all their attendant calamities. We are brought then to this startling but inevitable alternative. The natural life of an infant should be extinguished as soon as it is born, or the means should be provided to save that life from being a curse to its possessor; and therefore every State is bound to enact a code of laws legalizing and enforcing Infanticide, or a code of laws establishing Free Schools!

The three following propositions, then, describe the broad and ever-during foundation on which the Common School system of Massachusetts reposes:

The successive generations of men, taken collectively, constitute one great Commonwealth.

The property of this Commonwealth is pledged for the education of all its youth, up to such a point as will save them from poverty and vice, and prepare them for the adequate performance of their social and civil duties.

The successive holders of this property are trustees, bound to the faithful execution of their trust, by the most sacred obligations; because embezzlement and pillage from children and descendants are as criminal as the same offences when perpetrated against contemporaries.

Eleventh Annual Report (1847)

In the Eleventh Report *Mann argues the power of universal education to redeem the state from every manner of social vice and crime. "Having proved, then, in former Reports, by the testimony of wise and skilled men, that disease may be supplanted by health, bodily pain by enjoyment, and premature death by length of life, merely by the knowledge and practice of a few great physiological principles, . . . I propose to myself, in the residue of this Report, the still more delightful task of showing, by proofs equally unexceptionable and convincing, that the great body of vices and crimes which now sadden and torment the community, may be dislodged and driven out from amongst us, by such improvements in our present Common School system, as we are abundantly able immediately to make." Nowhere is the faith derived from phrenology and from his own Christian moralism more apparent than in this report. It is here that education becomes truly the "centre and circumference" of the "wheel of Progress."*

Twelfth Annual Report (1848)

The Twelfth Report *is Mann's summing-up; he wrote it after having won a seat in the United States Congress. It is also far and away the most inclusive and searching of the twelve documents. In it Mann draws together all of the themes of his earlier reports into one great credo of public education. The following pages include excerpts from each major section of his discussion as well as his lengthy commentary on the relation of church, state, and public school in a free society.*

Under the Providence of God, our means of education are the grand machinery by which the "raw material" of human nature can be worked up into inventors and discoverers, into skilled artisans and scientific farmers, into scholars and jurists, into the founders of benevolent institutions, and the great expounders of ethical and theological science. By means of early education, those embryos of talent may be quickened, which will solve the difficult problems of political and economical law; and by them, too, the genius may be kindled which will blaze forth in the Poets of Humanity. Our schools, far more than they have done, may supply the Presidents and Professors of Colleges, and Superintendents of Public Instruction, all over the land; and send, not only into our sister states, but across the Atlantic, the men of practical science, to superintend the construction of the great works of art. Here, too, may those judicial powers be developed and invigorated, which will make legal principles so clear and convincing as to prevent appeals to force; and, should the clouds of war ever lower over our country, some hero may be found,—the nursling of our schools, and ready to become the leader of our armies,—that best of all heroes, who will secure the glories of a peace, unstained by the magnificent murders of the battle-field. . . .

Without undervaluing any other human agency, it may be safely affirmed that the Common School, improved and energized, as it can easily be, may become the most effective and benignant of all the forces of civilization. Two reasons sustain this position. In the first place, there is a universality in its operation, which can be affirmed of no other institution whatever. If administered in the spirit of justice and conciliation, all the rising generation may be brought within the circle of its reformatory and elevating influences. And, in the second place, the materials upon which it operates are so pliant and ductile as to be susceptible of assuming a greater variety of forms than any other earthly work of the Creator. The inflexibility and ruggedness of the oak, when compared with the lithe sapling or the tender germ, are but feeble emblems to typify the docility of childhood, when contrasted with the obduracy and intractableness of man. It is these inherent advantages of the Common School, which, in our own State, have produced results so striking, from a system so imperfect, and an administration so feeble. In teaching the blind, and the deaf and dumb, in kindling the latent spark of intelligence that lurks in an idiot's mind, and in the more holy work of reforming abandoned and outcast children, education has proved what it can do, by glorious experiments. These wonders, it has done in its infancy, and with the lights of a limited experience; but, when its faculties shall be fully developed, when it shall be trained to wield its mighty energies for the protection of society against the giant vices which now invade and torment it;—against intemperance, avarice, war, slavery, bigotry, the woes of want and the wickedness of waste,—then, there will not be a height to which these enemies of the race can escape, which it will not scale, nor a Titan among them all, whom it will not slay.

I proceed, then, in endeavoring to show how the true business of the schoolroom connects itself, and becomes identical, with the great interests of society. The former is the infant, immature state of those interests; the latter, their developed, adult state. As "the child is father to the man," so may the training of the schoolroom expand into the institutions and fortunes of the State.

PHYSICAL EDUCATION

In the worldly prosperity of mankind, Health and Strength are indispensable ingredients. Reflect, for a moment, what an inroad upon the comfort of a family and its means of support, is a case of chronic sickness or debility, in a single one of its members. Should a farmer contract to support, and to continue to pay, his laborer, or a manufacturer his operative, whether able or unable to work, they would demand a serious abatement of wages, as a premium for the risk. But, whatever drawback a sick member would be to the pecuniary prosperity of a family, or a sick laborer to that of an employer bound to support him, just such a drawback is a sick or disabled member of the community to the financial prosperity of the State to which he belongs. The amount of loss consequent upon such sickness or disability may not be drawn out of the public treasury, but it is subtracted from the common property of the State, in a way still more injurious than if the same amount of gold were taken from the public coffers by warrant of the executive. Money, so taken, would be transferred to another hand. It would still exist. But the want of health and strength is a dead loss to the community; and, whenever the next valuation is taken, there will be a corresponding deficit in the aggregate of national property. Hence, every citizen, as such, is pecuniarily interested in the health and strength of all his fellow-citizens. It is right, therefore, that he should look upon them all, not only as a benevolent and Christian man would do, pitying and succoring their misfortunes; but he should look upon them, also, as a man of business;—as one who contributes, or is bound to contribute, to a reserved fund, from which all the non-producing sick and valetudinary are supported. . . .

Now modern science has made nothing more certain, than that both good and ill health are the direct result of causes, mainly within our own control. In other words, the health of the race is dependent upon the conduct of the race. The health of the individual is determined primarily by his parents; secondarily, by himself. The vigorous growth of the body, its strength and its activity, its powers of endurance, and its length of life, on the one hand; and dwarfishness, sluggishness, infirmity, and premature death, on the other, are all the subjects of unchangeable laws. These laws are ordained of God; but the knowledge of them is left to our diligence, and the observance of them to our free agency. These laws are very few; they are so simple that all can understand them, and so beautiful that the pleasure of contemplating them, even independent of their utility, is a tenfold reward for all the labor of their acquisition. The laws, I repeat, are few. The circumstances, however, under which they are to be applied, are exceedingly various and complicated. These circumstances embrace the almost infinite varieties of our daily life;—exercise and rest; sleeping and watching; eating, drinking, and abstinence; the affections and passions; exposure to vicissitudes of temperature, to dryness and humidity, to the effluvia and exhalations of dead animal or decaying vegetable matter;—in fine, they embrace all cases where excesses, indiscretions, or exposures, may induce disease; or where exercise, temperance, cleanliness, and pure air, may avert it. Hence it would be wholly impossible to write out any code of "Rules and Regulations," applicable to all cases. So, too, the occasions for applying the laws to new circumstances recur so continually that no man can have a Mentor at his side, in the form of a physician or physiologist, to direct his conduct in new emergencies. Even the most favored individual, in ninety-nine cases in a hundred, must prescribe for himself. And hence the uncompromising necessity that all children should be instructed in these laws; and not only instructed, but that they should receive such a *training*, during the whole course of pupilage, as to enlist the mighty forces of habit on the side of obedience; and that their judgment also should be so developed and matured that they will be able to discriminate between different combinations of circumstances, and to adapt, in each case, the regimen to the exigency. . . .

My general conclusion, then, under this head, is, that it is the duty of all the governing minds in society,—whether in office or out of it,—to diffuse a knowledge of these beautiful and beneficent laws of health and life, throughout the length and breadth of the State;—to popularize them; to make them, in the first place, the common acquisition of all, and, through education and custom, the common inheritance of all; so that the healthful habits naturally growing out of their observance, shall be inbred in the people; exemplified in the personal regimen of each individual; incorporated into the economy of every household; observable in all private dwellings, and in all public edifices, especially in those buildings which are erected by capitalists for the residence of their work-people, or for renting to the poorer classes; obeyed, by supplying cities with pure water; by providing public baths, public walks, and public squares; by rural cemeteries; by the drainage and sewerage of populous towns, and in whatever else may promote the general salubrity of the atmosphere;—in fine, by a religious observance of all those sanitary regulations with which modern science has blessed the world.

For this thorough diffusion of sanitary intelligence, the Common School is the only agency. It is, however, an adequate agency. Let Human Physiology be introduced as an indispensable branch of study into our Public Schools; let no teacher be approved who is not master of its leading principles, and of their applications to the varying circumstances of life; let all the older classes in the schools be regularly and rigidly examined upon this study by the school committees, and a speedy change would come over our personal habits, over our domestic usages, and over the public arrangements of society. Temperance and moderation would not be such strangers at the table. Fashion, like European sovereigns, if not compelled to abdicate and fly, would be forced to compromise for the continued possession of her throne, by the surrender to her subjects of many of their natural rights. A sixth order of architecture would be invented,—the Hygienic,—which, without subtracting at all from the beauty of any other order, would add a new element of utility to them all. The "Health Regulations" of cities would be issued in a revised code,—a code that would bear the scrutiny of science. And, as the result and reward of all, a race of men and women, loftier in stature, firmer in structure, fairer in form, and better able to perform the duties and bear the burdens of life, would revisit the earth. The minikin specimens of the race, who now go on dwindling and tapering from parent to child, would reäscend to manhood and womanhood. Just in proportion as the laws

84 THE REPUBLIC AND THE SCHOOL

of health and life were discovered and obeyed, would pain, disease, insanity, and untimely death, cease from among men. Consumption would remain; but it would be consumption in the active sense.

INTELLECTUAL EDUCATION, AS A MEANS OF REMOVING POVERTY, AND SECURING ABUNDANCE

Another cardinal object which the government of Massachusetts, and all the influential men in the State should propose to themselves, is the physical well-being of all the people,—the sufficiency, comfort, competence, of every individual, in regard to food, raiment, and shelter. And these necessaries and conveniences of life should be obtained by each individual for himself, or by each family for themselves, rather than accepted from the hand of charity, or extorted by poor-laws. It is not averred that this most desirable result can, in all instances, be obtained; but it is, nevertheless, the end to be aimed at. True statesmanship and true political economy, not less than true philanthropy, present this perfect theory as the goal, to be more and more closely approximated by our imperfect practice. The desire to achieve such a result cannot be regarded as an unreasonable ambition; for, though all mankind were well-fed, well-clothed, and well-housed, they might still be but half-civilized. . . .

According to the European theory, men are divided into classes,—some to toil and earn, others to seize and enjoy. According to the Massachusetts theory, all are to have an equal chance for earning, and equal security in the enjoyment of what they earn. The latter tends to equality of condition; the former to the grossest inequalities. Tried by any Christian standard of morals, or even by any of the better sort of heathen standards, can any one hesitate, for a moment, in declaring which of the two will produce the greater amount of human welfare; and which, therefore, is the more comformable to the Divine will? The European theory is blind to what constitutes the highest glory, as well as the highest duty, of a State. . . .

I suppose it to be the universal sentiment of all those who

THE EDUCATION OF FREE MEN

mingle any ingredient of benevolence with their notions on
Political Economy, that vast and overshadowing private fortunes are among the greatest dangers to which the happiness
of the people in a republic can be subjected. Such fortunes
would create a feudalism of a new kind; but one more oppressive and unrelenting than that of the Middle Ages.
The feudal lords in England, and on the continent, never
held their retainers in a more abject condition of servitude,
than the great majority of foreign manufacturers and capitalists hold their operatives and laborers at the present day.
The means employed are different, but the similarity in
results is striking. What force did then, money does now.
The villein of the Middle Ages had no spot of earth on
which he could live, unless one were granted to him by his
lord. The operative or laborer of the present day has no employment, and therefore no bread, unless the capitalist
will accept his services. The vassal had no shelter but such
as his master provided for him. Not one in five thousand
of English operatives, or farm laborers, is able to build or
own even a hovel; and therefore they must accept such
shelter as Capital offers them. The baron prescribed his own
terms to his retainers; those terms were peremptory, and the
serf must submit or perish. The British manufacturer or
farmer prescribes the rate of wages he will give to his work-
people; he reduces these wages under whatever pretext he
pleases; and they too have no alternative but submission or
starvation. In some respects, indeed, the condition of the
modern dependant is more forlorn than that of the corresponding serf class in former times. Some attributes of the
patriarchal relation did spring up between the lord and his
lieges, to soften the harsh relations subsisting between them.
Hence came some oversight of the condition of children,
some relief in sickness, some protection and support in the
decrepitude of age. But only in instances comparatively
few, have kindly offices smoothed the rugged relation between British Capital and British Labor. The children of
the work-people are abandoned to their fate; and, notwithstanding the privations they suffer, and the dangers they
threaten, no power in the realm has yet been able to secure
them an education; and when the adult laborer is prostrated
by sickness, or eventually worn out by toil and age, the poor-

house, which has all along been his destination, becomes his destiny.

Now two or three things will doubtless be admitted to be true, beyond all controversy, in regard to Massachusetts. By its industrial condition, and its business operations, it is exposed, far beyond any other state in the Union, to the fatal extremes of overgrown wealth and desperate poverty. Its population is far more dense than that of any other state. It is four or five times more dense than the average of all the other states, taken together; and density of population has always been one of the proximate causes of social inequality. According to population and territorial extent, there is far more capital in Massachusetts,—capital which is movable, and instantaneously available,—than in any other state in the Union; and probably both these qualifications respecting population and territory could be omitted without endangering the truth of the assertion. It has been recently stated, in a very respectable public journal, on the authority of a writer conversant with the subject, that, from the last of June, 1846, to the 1st of August, 1848, the amount of money invested, by the citizens of Massachusetts, "in manufacturing cities, railroads, and other improvements," is "fifty-seven millions of dollars, of which more than fifty has been paid in and expended." The dividends to be received by the citizens of Massachusetts from June, 1848, to April, 1849, are estimated, by the same writer, at ten millions, and the annual increase of capital at "little short of twenty-two millions." If this be so, are we not in danger of naturalizing and domesticating among ourselves those hideous evils which are always engendered between Capital and Labor, when all the capital is in the hands of one class, and all the labor is thrown upon another?

Now, surely, nothing but Universal Education can counter-work this tendency to the domination of capital and the servility of labor. If one class possesses all the wealth and the education, while the residue of society is ignorant and poor, it matters not by what name the relation between them may be called; the latter, in fact and in truth, will be the servile dependants and subjects of the former. But if education be equably diffused, it will draw property after it, by the strongest of all attractions; for such a thing never did happen, and never can happen, as that an intelligent and practical body of men should be permanently poor. Property and labor, in different classes, are essentially antagonistic; but property and labor, in the same class, are essentially fraternal. The people of Massachusetts have, in some degree, appreciated the truth, that the unexampled prosperity of the State,—its comfort, its competence, its general intelligence and virtue,—is attributable to the education, more or less perfect, which all its people have received; but are they sensible of a fact equally important?—namely, that it is to this same education that two thirds of the people are indebted for not being, to-day, the vassals of as severe a tyranny, in the form of capital, as the lower classes of Europe are bound to in the form of brute force.

Education, then, beyond all other devices of human origin, is the great equalizer of the conditions of men—the balance-wheel of the social machinery. I do not here mean that it so elevates the moral nature as to make men disdain and abhor the oppression of their fellow-men. This idea pertains to another of its attributes. But I mean that it gives each man the independence and the means, by which he can resist the selfishness of other men. It does better than to disarm the poor of their hostility towards the rich; it prevents being poor. Agrarianism is the revenge of poverty against wealth. The wanton destruction of the property of others,—the burning of hay-ricks and corn-ricks, the demolition of machinery, because it supersedes hand-labor, the sprinkling of vitriol on rich dresses,—is only agrarianism run mad. Education prevents both the revenge and the madness. On the other hand, a fellow-feeling for one's class or caste is the common instinct of hearts not wholly sunk in selfish regards for person, or for family. The spread of education, by enlarging the cultivated class or caste, will open a wider area over which the social feelings will expand; and, if this education should be universal and complete, it would do more than all things else to obliterate factitious distinctions in society.

The main idea set forth in the creeds of some political reformers, or revolutionizers, is, that some people are poor *because* others are rich. This idea supposes a fixed amount of property in the community, which, by fraud or force, or arbitrary law, is unequally divided among men; and the problem presented for solution is, how to transfer a portion of this property from those who are supposed to have too much, to those who feel and know that they have too little. At this point, both their theory and their expectation of reform stop. But the beneficent power of education would not be exhausted, even though it should peaceably abolish all the miseries that spring from the coëxistence, side by side, of enormous wealth and squalid want. It has a higher function. Beyond the power of diffusing old wealth, it has the prerogative of creating new. It is a thousand times more lucrative than fraud; and adds a thousand fold more to a nation's resources than the most successful conquests. Knaves and robbers can obtain only what was before possessed by others. But education creates or develops new treasures,— treasures not before possessed or dreamed of by any one. . . .

If a savage will learn how to swim, he can fasten a dozen pounds' weight to his back, and transport it across a narrow river, or other body of water of moderate width. If he will invent an axe, or other instrument, by which to cut down a tree, he can use the tree for a float, and one of its limbs for a paddle, and can thus transport many times the former weight, many times the former distance. Hollowing out his log, he will increase, what may be called, its tonnage,—or, rather, its *poundage*,—and, by sharpening its ends, it will cleave the water both more easily and more swiftly. Fastening several trees together, he makes a raft, and thus increases the buoyant power of his embryo water-craft. Turning up the ends of small poles, or using knees of timber instead of straight pieces, and grooving them together, or filling up the interstices between them, in some other way, so as to make them water-tight, he brings his rude raft literally into *ship-shape*. Improving upon hull below and rigging above, he makes a proud merchantman, to be wafted by the winds from continent to continent. But, even this does not content the adventurous naval architect. He frames iron arms for his ship; and, for oars, affixes iron wheels, capable of swift revolution, and stronger than the strong sea. Into iron-walled cavities in her bosom, he puts iron organs of massive structure and strength, and of cohesion insoluble by fire. Within these, he kindles a small volcano; and then, like a sentient and rational existence, this wonderful creation of his hands cleaves oceans, breasts tides, defies tempests, and bears its living and jubilant freight around the globe. Now, take away intelligence from the ship-builder, and the steam-ship,—that miracle of human art,—falls back into a floating log; the log itself is lost; and the savage swimmer, bearing his dozen pounds on his back, alone remains.

And so it is, not in one department only, but in the whole circle of human labors. The annihilation of the sun would no more certainly be followed by darkness, than the extinction of human intelligence would plunge the race at once into the weakness and helplessness of barbarism. To have created such beings as we are, and to have placed them in this world, without the light of the sun, would be no more cruel than for a government to suffer its laboring classes to grow up without knowledge. . . .

For the creation of wealth, then,—for the existence of a wealthy people and a wealthy nation,—intelligence is the grand condition. The number of improvers will increase, as the intellectual constituency, if I may so call it, increases. In former times, and in most parts of the world even at the present day, not one man in a million has ever had such a development of mind, as made it possible for him to become a contributor to art or science. Let this development precede, and contributions, numberless, and of inestimable value, will be sure to follow. That Political Economy, therefore, which busies itself about capital and labor, supply and demand, interest and rents, favorable and unfavorable balances of trade; but leaves out of account the element of a wide-spread mental development, is nought but stupendous folly. The greatest of all the arts in political economy is, to change a consumer into a producer; and the next greatest is to increase the producer's producing power;—an end to be directly attained, by increasing his intelligence. . . .

POLITICAL EDUCATION

The necessity of general intelligence,—that is, of education, (for I use the terms as substantially synonymous; because general intelligence can never exist without general education, and general education will be sure to produce general intelligence,)—the necessity of general intelligence, under a republican form of government, like most other very important truths, has become a very trite one. It is so trite, indeed, as to have lost much of its force by its familiarity. Almost all the champions of education seize upon this argument, first of all; because it is so simple as to be understood by the ignorant, and so strong as to convince the sceptical. Nothing would be easier than to follow in the train of so many writers, and to demonstrate, by logic, by history, and by the nature of the case, that a republican form of government, without intelligence in the people, must be, on a vast scale, what a mad-house, without superintendent or keepers, would be, on a small one;—the despotism of a few succeeded by universal anarchy, and anarchy by despotism, with no change but from bad to worse. Want of space and time alike forbid me to attempt any full development of the merits of this theme; but yet, in the closing one of a series of reports, partaking somewhat of the nature of a summary of former arguments, an omission of this topic would suggest to the comprehensive mind the idea of incompleteness.

That the affairs of a great nation or state are exceedingly complicated and momentous, no one will dispute. Nor will it be questioned that the degree of intelligence that superintends, should be proportioned to the magnitude of the interests superintended. He who scoops out a wooden dish needs less skill than the maker of a steam-engine or a telescope. The dealer in small wares requires less knowledge than the merchant who exports and imports to and from all quarters of the globe. An ambassador cannot execute his functions with the stock of attainments or of talents sufficient for a parish clerk. Indeed, it is clear, that the want of *adequate* intelligence,—of intelligence *commensurate* with the nature of the duties to be performed,—will bring ruin or disaster upon any department. A merchant loses his intelligence, and he becomes a bankrupt. A lawyer loses his intelligence, and he forfeits all the interests of his clients. Intelligence abandons a physician, and his patients die, with more than the pains of natural dissolution. Should judges upon the bench be bereft of this guide, what havoc would be made of the property and the innocence of men! Let this counsellor be taken from executive officers, and the penalties due to the wicked would be visited upon the righteous, while the rewards and immunities of the righteous would be bestowed upon the guilty. And so, should intelligence desert the halls of legislation, weakness, rashness, contradiction, and error, would glare out from every page of the statute book. Now, as a republican government represents almost all interests, whether social, civil or military, the necessity of a degree of intelligence adequate to the due administration of them all, is so self-evident, that a bare statement is the best argument.

But in the possession of this attribute of intelligence, elective legislators will never far surpass their electors. By a natural law, like that which regulates the equilibrium of fluids, elector and elected, appointer and appointee, tend to the same level. It is not more certain that a wise and enlightened constituency will refuse to invest a reckless and profligate man with office, or discard him if accidentally chosen, than it is that a foolish or immoral constituency will discard or eject a wise man. This law of assimilation, between the choosers and the chosen, results, not only from the fact that the voter originally selects his representative according to the affinities of good or of ill, of wisdom or of folly, which exist between them; but if the legislator enacts or favors a law which is too wise for the constituent to understand, or too just for him to approve, the next election will set him aside as certainly as if he had made open merchandise of the dearest interests of the people, by perjury and for a bribe. And if the infinitely Just and Good, in giving laws to the Jews, recognized the "hardness of their hearts," how much more will an earthly ruler recognize the baseness or wickedness of the people, when his heart is as hard as theirs! In a republican government, legislators are a mirror reflecting the moral countenance of their constituents. And hence it is, that the establishment of a republican government, without well-appointed and effcient means for the universal education of the people, is the most rash and fool-hardy experiment ever tried by man. Its fatal results may not be immediately developed,—they may not follow as the thunder follows the lightning,—for time is an element in maturing them, and the calamity is too great to be prepared in a day; but, like the slow-accumulating avalanche, they will grow more terrific by delay, and, at length, though it may be at a late hour, will overwhelm with ruin whatever lies athwart their path. It may be an easy thing to make a Republic; but it is a very laborious thing to make Republicans; and woe to the republic that rests upon no better foundations than ignorance, selfishness, and passion. Such a republic may grow in numbers and in wealth. As an avaricious man adds acres to his lands, so its rapacious government may increase its own darkness by annexing provinces and states to its ignorant domain. Its armies may be invincible, and its fleets may strike terror into nations on the opposite sides of the globe, at the same hour. Vast in its extent, and enriched with all the prodigality of nature, it may possess every capacity and opportunity of being great, and of doing good. But if such a Republic be devoid of intelligence, it will only the more closely resemble an obscene giant who has waxed strong in his youth, and grown wanton in his strength; whose brain has been developed only in the region of the appetites and passions, and not in the organs of reason and conscience; and who, therefore, is boastful of his bulk alone, and glories in the weight of his heel and in the destruction of his arm. Such a republic, with all its noble capacities for beneficence, will rush with the speed of a whirlwind to an ignominious end; and all good men of after-times would be fain to weep over its downfall, did not their scorn and contempt at its folly and its wickedness, repress all sorrow for its fate. . . .

However elevated the moral character of a constituency may be; however well informed in matters of general science or history, yet they must, if citizens of a Republic, understand something of the true nature and functions of the government under which they live. That any one who is to participate in the government of a country, when he becomes a man, should receive no instruction respecting the nature and functions of the government he is afterwards to administer, is a political solecism. In all nations, hardly excepting the most rude and barbarous, the future sovereign receives some training which is supposed to fit him for the exercise of the powers and duties of his anticipated station. Where, by force of law, the government devolves upon the heir, while yet in a state of legal infancy, some regency, or other substitute, is appointed, to act in his stead, until his arrival at mature age; and, in the meantime, he is subjected to such a course of study and discipline, as will tend to prepare him, according to the political theory of the time and the place, to assume the reins of authority at the appointed age. If, in England, or in the most enlightened European monarchies, it would be a proof of restored barbarism, to permit the future sovereign to grow up without any knowledge of his duties,—and who can doubt that it would be such a proof,—then, surely, it would be not less a proof of restored, or of never-removed barbarism, amongst us, to empower any individual to use the elective franchise, without preparing him for so momentous a trust. Hence, the constitution of the United States, and of our own State, should be made a study in our Public Schools. The partition of the powers of government into the three co-ordinate branches,—legislative, judicial, and executive,—with the duties appropriately devolving upon each; the mode of electing or of appointing all officers, with the reason on which it was founded; and, especially, the duty of every citizen, in a government of laws, to appeal to the courts for redress, in all cases of alleged wrong, instead of undertaking to vindicate his own rights by his own arm; and, in a government where the people are the acknowledged sources of power, the duty of changing laws and rulers by an appeal to the ballot, and not by rebellion, should be taught to all the children until they are fully understood.

Had the obligations of the future citizen been sedulously inculcated upon all the children of this Republic, would the patriot have had to mourn over so many instances, where the voter, not being able to accomplish his purpose by voting, has proceeded to accomplish it by violence; where, agreeing with his fellow-citizens, to use the machinery of the ballot, he makes a tacit reservation, that, if that machinery does not move according to his pleasure, he will wrest or break it? If the responsibleness and value of the elective franchise were duly appreciated, the day of our State and National elections would be among the most solemn and religious days in the calendar. Men would approach them, not only with preparation and solicitude, but with the sobriety and solemnity, with which discreet and religious-minded men meet the great crises of life. No man would throw away his vote, through caprice or wantonness, any more than he would throw away his estate, or sell his family into bondage. No man would cast his vote through malice or revenge, any more than a good surgeon would amputate a limb, or a good navigator sail through perilous straits, under the same criminal passions.

But, perhaps, it will be objected, that the constitution is subject to different readings, or that the policy of different administrations has become the subject of party strife; and, therefore, if any thing of constitutional or political law is introduced into our schools, there is danger that teachers will be chosen on account of their affinities to this or that political party; or that teachers will feign affinities which they do not feel, in order that they may be chosen; and so each schoolroom will at length become a miniature political club-room, exploding with political resolves, or flaming out with political addresses, prepared, by beardless boys, in scarcely legible hand-writing, and in worse grammar.

With the most limited exercise of discretion, all apprehensions of this kind are wholly groundless. There are different readings of the constitution, it is true; and there are partisan topics which agitate the country from side to side; but the controverted points, compared with those about which there is no dispute, do not bear the proportion of one to a hundred. And what is more, no man is qualified, or can be qualified, to discuss the disputable questions, unless previously and thoroughly versed in those questions, about which there is no dispute. In the terms and principles common to all, and recognized by all, is to be found the only common medium of language and of idea, by which the parties can become intelligible to each other; and there, too, is the only common ground, whence the arguments of the disputants can be drawn.

It is obvious, on the other hand, that if the tempest of political strife were to be let loose upon our Common Schools, they would be overwhelmed with sudden ruin. Let it be once understood, that the schoolroom is a legitimate theatre for party politics, and with what violence will hostile partisans struggle to gain possession of the stage, and to play their parts upon it! Nor will the stage be the only scene of gladiatorial contests. These will rage in all the avenues that lead to it. A preliminary advantage, indispensable to ultimate success, will be the appointment of a teacher of the true faith. As the great majority of the schools in the State are now organized, this can be done only by electing a prudential committee, who will make what he calls political soundness paramount to all other considerations of fitness. Thus, after petty skirmishings among neighbors, the fierce encounter will begin in the district's primary assembly,—in the schoolroom itself. This contest being over, the election of the superintending, or town's committee, must be determined in the same way, and this will bring together the combustibles of each district, to burn with an intenser and a more devouring flame, in the town meeting. It is very possible, nay, not at all improbable, that the town may be of one political complexion, while a majority of the districts are of the opposite. Who shall moderate the fury of these conflicting elements, when they rage against each other; and who shall save the dearest interests of the children from being consumed in the fierce combustion? If parents find that their children are indoctrinated into what they call political heresies, will they not withdraw them from the school; and, if they withdraw them from the school, will they not resist all appropriations to support a school from which they derive no benefit?

But, could the schools, themselves, survive these dangers for a single year, it would be only to encounter others still more perilous. Why should not the same infection that poisons all the relations of the schoolroom, spread itself abroad, and mingle with all questions of external organization and arrangement? Why should not political hostility cause the dismemberment of districts, already too small; or, what would work equal injury, prevent the union of districts, whose power of usefulness would be doubled by a combination of their resources? What better could be expected, than that one set of school books should be expelled, and another introduced, as they might be supposed, however remotely, to favor one party or the other; or, as the authors of the books might belong to one party or the other? And who could rely upon the reports, or even the statistics of a committee, chosen by partisan votes, goaded on by partisan impulses, and responsible to partisan domination; and this, too, without any opportunity of control or check from the minority? Nay, if the schools could survive long enough to meet the crisis, why should not any and every measure be taken, either to maintain an existing political ascendancy, or to recover a lost one, in a school district, or in a town, which has even been taken by unscrupulous politicians, to maintain or to recover an ascendancy at the polls? Into a district, or into a town, voters may be introduced from abroad, to turn the scale. An employer may dismiss the employed, for their refusal to submit to his dictation; or make the bread that is given to the poor man's children, perform the double office of payment for labor to be performed, and of a bribe for principle to be surrendered. And, beyond all this, if the imagination can conceive any thing more deplorable than this, what kind of political doctrines would be administered to the children, amid the vicissitudes of party domination,— their alternations of triumph and defeat? This year, under the ascendancy of one side, the constitution declares one thing; and commentaries, glosses, and the authority of distinguished names, all ratify and confirm its decisions. But victory is a fickle goddess. Next year, the vanquished triumph; and constitution, gloss, and authority, make that sound doctrine, which was pestilent error before, and that false, which was true. Right and wrong have changed sides. The children must now join in chorus to denounce what they had been taught to reverence before, and to reverence what they had been taught to denounce. In the mean time, those great principles, which, according to Cicero, are the same at Rome and at Athens, the same now and forever;— and which, according to Hooker, have their seat in the bosom of God, become the fittest emblems of chance and change.

Long, however, before this series of calamities would exhaust itself upon our schools, these schools themselves would cease to be. The plough-share would have turned up their foundations. Their history would have been brought to a close,—a glorious and ascending history, until struck down by the hand of political parricide; then, suddenly falling with a double ruin,—with death, and with ignominy.

But to avoid such a catastrophe, shall all teaching, relative to the nature of our government, be banished from our schools; and shall our children be permitted to grow up in entire ignorance of the political history of their country? In the schools of a republic, shall the children be left without any distinct knowledge of the nature of a republican government; or only with such knowledge as they may pick up from angry political discussions, or from party newspapers; from caucus speeches, or Fourth of July orations,—the Apocrypha of Apocrypha?

Surely, between these extremes, there must be a medium not difficult to be found. And is not this the middle course, which all sensible and judicious men, all patriots, and all genuine republicans, must approve?—namely, that those articles in the creed of republicanism, which are accepted by all, believed in by all, and which form the common basis of our political faith, shall be taught to all. But when the teacher, in the course of his lessons or lectures on the fundamental law, arrives at a controverted text, he is either to read it without comment or remark; or, at most, he is only to say that the passage is the subject of disputation, and that the schoolroom is neither the tribunal to adjudicate, nor the forum to discuss it.

Such being the rule established by common consent, and such the practice, observed with fidelity under it, it will come to be universally understood, that political proselytism is no function of the school; but that all indoctrination into matters of controversy between hostile political parties is to be elsewhere sought for, and elsewhere imparted. Thus, may all the children of the Commonwealth receive instruction in the great essentials of political knowledge,—in those elementary ideas without which they will never be able to investigate more recondite and debatable questions;—thus, will the only practicable method be adopted for discovering new truths, and for discarding,—instead of perpetuating,—old errors; and thus, too, will that pernicious race of intolerant zealots, whose whole faith may be summed up in two articles,—that they, themselves, are always infallibly right, and that all dissenters are certainly wrong,—be extinguished,—extinguished, not by violence, nor by proscription, but by the more copious inflowing of the light of truth.

MORAL EDUCATION

Moral education is a primal necessity of social existence. The unrestrained passions of men are not only homicidal, but suicidal; and a community without a conscience would soon extinguish itself. Even with a natural conscience, how often has Evil triumphed over Good! From the beginning of time, Wrong has followed Right, as the shadow the substance. As the relations of men became more complex, and the business of the world more extended, new opportunities and new temptations for wrong-doing have been created. With the endearing relations of parent and child, came also the possibility of infanticide and parricide; and the first domestic altar that brothers ever reared was stained with fratricidal blood. Following close upon the obligations to truth, came falsehood and perjury, and closer still upon the duty of obedience to the Divine law, came disobedience. With the existence of private relations between men, came fraud; and with the existence of public relations between nations, came aggression, war, and slavery. And so, just in proportion as the relations of life became more numerous, and the interests of society more various and manifold, the range of possible and of actual offences has been continually enlarging. As for every new substance there may be a new shadow, so for every new law there may be a new transgression. No form of the precious metals has ever been used which dishonest men have not counterfeited; and no kind of artificial currency has ever been legalized which rogues have not forged. The government sees the evils that come from the use of intoxicating drinks, and prohibits their sale; but unprincipled men pander to depraved appetites, and gather a harvest of dishonest profits. Instead of licensing lotteries, and deriving a revenue from the sale of tickets, the State forbids the mischievous traffic; but while law-abiding men disdain to practice an illicit trade, knavish brokers, by means of the prohibition itself, secure a monopoly of the sales, and pocket the infamous gain. The government imposes duties on imported goods; smugglers evade the law, and bring goods into the country clandestinely; or perjurers swear to false invoices, and escape the payment of duty, and thus secure to themselves the double advantage of increased sales, and enhanced profits upon what is sold. Science prepares a new medicine to heal or alleviate the diseases of men; crime adulterates it, or prepares, as a substitute, some cheap poison that resembles it, and can be sold instead of it. A benefactor of the race discovers an agent which has the marvellous power to suspend consciousness, and take away the susceptibility of pain; a villain uses it to rob men or pollute women. Houses are built; the incendiary burns them, that he may purloin the smallest portion of their goods. The press is invented to spread intelligence; but libellers use it to give wings to slander. And, so, throughout all the infinitely complex and ramified relations of society, wherever there is a right there may be a wrong; and wherever a law is made to repress the wrong, it may be evaded by artifice or overborne by violence. In fine, all means and laws designed to repress injustice and crime, give occasion to new injustice and crime. For every lock that is made, a false key is made to pick it; and for every Paradise that is created, there is a Satan who would scale its walls. . . .

Against these social vices, in all ages of the world, the admonitions of good men have been directed. The moralist has exposed their deformity in his didactic page; the satirist has chastised them in his pungent verse; the dramatist has held them up to ridicule on the mimic stage; and, to some extent, the Christian minister has exhibited their gross repugnancy to the character of a disciple of Jesus. Still they continue to exist; and,—to say nothing of heathen nations, —the moral condition of all Christendom is, in this respect, like the physical condition of one of the nations that compose it;—that extraordinary people, I mean, whose dwellings, whose flocks, whose agriculture, whose merchandise, and who, themselves, are below the level of the ocean; and against them, at all times, this ocean rages, and lifts itself up; and whenever or wherever it can find a breach, or make one, it rushes in, and overwhelms men and their possessions in one common inundation. Even so, like a weltering flood, do immoralities and crimes break over all moral barriers, destroying and profaning the securities and the sanctities of life. Now, how best shall this deluge be repelled? What mighty power, or combination of powers, can prevent its inrushing, or narrow the sweep of its ravages?

The race has existed long enough to try many experiments for the solution of this greatest problem ever submitted to its hands; and the race has experimented, without stint of time or circumscription of space, to mar or modify legitimate results. Mankind have tried despotisms, monarchies, and republican forms of government. They have tried the extremes of anarchy and of autocracy. They have tried Draconian codes of law; and, for the lightest offences, have extenguished the life of the offender. They have established theological standards, claiming for them the sanction of Divine authority, and the attributes of a perfect and infallible law; and then they have imprisoned, burnt, massacred, not individuals only, but whole communities at a time, for not bowing down to idols which ecclesiastical authority had set up. These and other great systems of measures have been adopted as barriers against error and guilt; they have been extended over empires, prolonged through centuries, and administered with terrible energy; and yet the great ocean of vice and crime overleaps every embankment, pours down upon our heads, saps the foundations under our feet, and sweeps away the securities of social order, of property, liberty, and life.

At length, these experiments have been so numerous, and all of them have terminated so disastrously, that a body of men has risen up, in later times, powerful in influence, and not inconsiderable in numbers, who, if I may use a mercantile phrase, would abandon the world as a total loss;—who mock at the idea of its having a benevolent or even an intelligent Author or Governor; and who, therefore, would give over the race to the dominion of chance, or to that of their own licentious passions, whose rule would be more fatal than chance.

But to all doubters, disbelievers, or despairers, in human progress, it may still be said, there is one experiment which has never yet been tried. It is an experiment which, even before its inception, offers the highest authority for its ultimate success. Its formula is intelligible to all; and it is as legible as though written in starry letters on an azure sky. It is expressed in these few and simple words:—*"Train up a child in the way he should go, and when he is old he will not depart from it."* This declaration is positive. If the conditions are complied with, it makes no provision for a failure. Though pertaining to morals, yet, if the terms of the direction are observed, there is no more reason to doubt the result, than there would be in an optical or a chemical experiment.

But this experiment has never yet been tried. Education has never yet been brought to bear with one hundredth part of its potential force, upon the natures of children, and, through them, upon the character of men, and of the race. In all the attempts to reform mankind which have hitherto been made, whether by changing the frame of government, by aggravating or softening the severity of the penal code, or by substituting a government-created, for a God-created religion;—in all these attempts, the infantile and youthful mind, its amenability to influences, and the enduring and self-operating character of the influences it receives, have been almost wholly unrecognized. Here, then, is a new agency, whose powers are but just beginning to be understood, and whose mighty energies, hitherto, have been but feebly invoked; and yet, from our experience, limited and imperfect as it is, we do know that, far beyond any other earthly instrumentality, it is comprehensive and decisive. . . .

RELIGIOUS EDUCATION

. . . On this subject, I propose to speak with freedom and plainness, and more at length than I should feel required to do, but for the peculiar circumstances in which I have been placed. It is matter of notoriety, that the views of the Board of Education,—and my own, perhaps still more than those of the Board,—on the subject of religious instruction in our Public Schools, have been subjected to animadversion. Grave charges have been made against us, that our purpose was to exclude religion; and to exclude that, too, which is the common exponent of religion,—the Bible,—from the Common Schools of the State; or, at least, to derogate from its authority, and destroy its influence in them. Whatever prevalence a suspicion of the truth of these imputations may have heretofore had, I have reason to believe that further inquiry and examination have done much to disabuse the too credulous recipients of so groundless a charge. Still, amongst a people so commendably sensitive on the subject of religion, as are the people of Massachusetts, any suspicion of irreligious tendencies, will greatly prejudice any cause, and, so far as any cause may otherwise have the power of doing good, will greatly impair that power.

It is known, too, that our noble system of Free Schools for the whole people, is strenuously opposed;—by a few persons in our own State, and by no inconsiderable numbers in some of the other states of this Union;—and that a rival system of "Parochial" or "Sectarian Schools," is now urged upon the public by a numerous, a powerful, and a well-organized body of men. It has pleased the advocates of this rival system, in various public addresses, in reports, and through periodicals devoted to their cause, to denounce our system as irreligious and anti-Christian. They do not trouble themselves to describe what our system is, but adopt a more summary way to forestall public opinion against it, by using general epithets of reproach, and signals of alarm.

In this age of the world, it seems to me that no student of history, or observer of mankind, can be hostile to the precepts and the doctrines of the Christian religion, or opposed to any institutions which expound and exemplify them; and no man who thinks, as I cannot but think, respecting the enduring elements of character, whether public or private, can be willing to have his name mentioned while he is living, or remembered when he is dead, as opposed to religious instruction, and Bible instruction for the young. In making this final Report, therefore, I desire to vindicate my conduct from the charges that have been made against it; and, so far as the Board has been implicated in these charges, to leave my testimony on record for their exculpation. Indeed, on this point, the Board and myself must be justified or condemned together; for I do not believe they would have enabled me, by their annual reëlections, to carry forward any plan for excluding either the Bible or religious instruction from the schools; and had the Board required me to execute such a purpose, I certainly should have given them the earliest opportunity to appoint my successor. I desire, also, to vindicate the system with which I have been so long and so intimately connected, not only from the aspersion, but from the suspicion, of being an irreligious, or anti-Christian, or an un-Christian system. I know, full well, that it is unlike the systems which prevail in Great Britain, and in many of the continental nations of Europe, where the Established Church controls the education of the young, in order to keep itself established. But this is presumptive evidence in its favor, rather than against it.

All the schemes ever devised by governments, to secure the prevalence and permanence of religion among the people, however variant in form they may have been, are substantially resolvable into two systems. One of these systems holds the regulation and control of the religious belief of the people to be one of the functions of government, like the command of the army or the navy, or the establishment of courts, or the collection of revenues. According to the other system, religious belief is a matter of individual and parental concern; and, while the government furnishes all practicable facilities for the independent formation of that belief, it exercises no authority to prescribe, or coercion to enforce it. The former is the system, which, with very few exceptions, has prevailed throughout Christendom, for fifteen hundred years. Our own government is almost a solitary example among the nations of the earth, where freedom of opinion, and the inviolability of conscience, have been even theoretically recognized by the law. . . .

The very terms, *Public School,* and *Common School,* bear upon their face, that they are schools which the children of the entire community may attend. Every man, not on the pauper list, is taxed for their support. But he is not taxed to support them as special religious institutions; if he were, it would satisfy, at once, the largest definition of a Religious Establishment. But he is taxed to support them, as a *preventive* means against dishonesty, against fraud, and against violence; on the same principle that he is taxed to support criminal courts as a *punitive* means against the same offences. He is taxed to support schools, on the same principle that he is taxed to support paupers; because a child without education is poorer and more wretched than a man without bread. He is taxed to support schools, on the same principle that he would be taxed to defend the nation against foreign invasion, or against rapine committed by a foreign foe; because the general prevalence of ignorance, superstition, and vice, will breed Goth and Vandal at home, more fatal to the public well-being, than any Goth or Vandal from abroad. And, finally, he is taxed to support schools, because they are the most effective means of developing and training those powers and faculties in a child, by which, when he becomes a man, he may understand what his highest interests and his highest duties are; and may be, in fact, and not in name only, a free agent. The elements of a political education are not bestowed upon any school child, for the purpose of making him vote with this or that political party, when he becomes of age; but for the purpose of enabling him to choose for himself, with which party he will vote. So the religious education which a child receives at school, is not imparted to him, for the purpose of making him join this or that denomination, when he arrives at years of discretion, but for the purpose of enabling him to judge for himself, according to the dictates of his own reason and conscience, what his religious obligations are, and whither they lead. But if a man is taxed to support a school, where religious doctrines are inculcated which he believes to be false, and which he believes that God condemns; then he is excluded from the school by the Divine law, at the same time that he is compelled to support it by the human law. This is a double wrong. It is politically wrong, because, if such a man educates his children at all, he must educate them elsewhere, and thus pay two taxes, while some of his neighbors pay less than their due proportion of one; and it is religiously wrong, because he is constrained, by human power, to promote what he believes the Divine Power forbids. The principle involved in such a course is pregnant with all tyrannical consequences. It is broad enough to sustain any claim of ecclesiastical domination, ever made in the darkest ages of the world. Every religious persecution, since the time of Constantine, may find its warrant in it, and can be legitimately defended upon it. If a man's estate may be taken from him to pay for teaching a creed which he believes to be false, his children can be taken from him to be taught the same creed; and he, too, may be punished to any extent, for not voluntarily surrendering both his estate and his offspring. If his children can be compulsorily taken and taught to believe a creed which the parent disbelieves, then the parent can be compulsorily taken and made to subscribe the same creed. And, in regard to the extent of the penalties which may be invoked to compel conformity, there is no stopping-place between taking a penny and inflicting perdition. It is only necessary to call a man's reason and conscience and religious faith, by the name of recusancy, or contumacy, or heresy, and so to inscribe them on the statute book; and then the non-conformist or dissenter may be subdued by steel, or cord, or fire; by anathema and excommunication in this life, and the terrors of endless perdition in the next. Surely, that system cannot be an irreligious, an anti-Christian, or an un-Christian one, whose first and cardinal principle it is, to recognize and protect the highest and dearest of all human interests, and of all human rights. . . .

It is still easier to prove that the Massachusetts school system is not anti-Christian nor un-Christian. The Bible is the acknowledged expositor of Christianity. In strictness, Christianity has no other authoritative expounder. This Bible is in our Common Schools, by common consent. Twelve years ago, it was not in all the schools. Contrary to the genius of our government, if not contrary to the express letter of the law, it had been used for sectarian purposes,—to prove one sect to be right, and others to be wrong. Hence, it had been excluded from the schools of some towns, by an express vote. But since the law and the reasons on which it is founded, have been more fully explained and better understood; and since sectarian instruction has, to a great extent, ceased to be given, the Bible has been restored. I am not aware of the existence of a single town in the State, in whose schools it is not now introduced, either by a direct vote of the school committee, or by such general desire and acquiescence, as supersede the necessity of a vote. In all my intercourse, for twelve years, whether personal or by letter, with all the school officers in the State, and with tens of thousands of individuals in it, I have never heard an objection made to the use of the Bible in school, except in one or two instances; and, in those cases, the objection was put upon the ground, that daily familiarity with the book, in school, would tend to impair a reverence for it.

If the Bible, then, is the exponent of Christianity; if the Bible contains the communications, precepts, and doctrines, which make up the religious system, called and known as Christianity; if the Bible makes known those truths, which, according to the faith of Christians, are able to make men wise unto salvation; and if this Bible is in the schools, how can it be said that Christianity is excluded from the schools; or how can it be said that the school system, which adopts and uses the Bible, is an anti-Christian, or an un-Christian system? If that which is the acknowledged exponent and basis of Christianity is in the schools, by what tergiversation in language, or paralogism in logic, can Christianity be said to be shut out from the schools? If the Old Testament were in the schools, could a Jew complain, that Judaism was excluded from them? If the Koran were read regularly and reverently in the schools, could a Mahomedan say that Mahomedanism was excluded? Or, if the Mormon Bible were in the schools, could it be said that Mormonism was excluded from them?

Is it not, indeed, too plain, to require the formality of a syllogism, that if any man's creed is to be found in the Bible, and the Bible is in the schools, then that man's creed is in the schools? This seems even plainer than the proposition, that two and two make four;—that is, we can conceive of a creature so low down in the scale of intelligence, that he could not see what sum would be produced by adding two and two together, who still could not fail to see, that, if a certain system, called Christianity, were contained in, and inseparable from, a certain book called the Bible, then wherever the Bible might go, there the system of Christianity must be. . . .

And further; our law explicit and solemnly enjoins it upon all teachers, without any exception, "to exert their best endeavors, to impress on the minds of children and youth committed to their care and instruction, the principles of piety, justice, and a sacred regard to truth, love to their country, humanity and universal benevolence, sobriety, industry, and frugality, chastity, moderation, and temperance, and those other virtues which are the ornament of human society, and the basis upon which a republican constitution is founded." Are not these virtues and graces part and parcel of Christianity? In other words, can there be Christianity without them? While these virtues and these duties towards God and man, are inculcated in our schools, any one who says that the schools are anti-Christian or un-Christian, expressly affirms that his own system of Christianity does not embrace any one of this radiant catalogue; that it rejects them all; that it embraces their opposites!

And further still; our system makes it the express duty of all the "resident ministers of the Gospel" to bring all the children within the moral and Christian inculcations above enumerated; so that he who avers that our system is an anti-Christian or an un-Christian one, avers that it is both anti-Christian and un-Christian for a "minister OF THE GOSPEL to promote, or labor to diffuse, the moral attributes and excellences, which the statute so earnestly enjoins.

So far, the argument has been of an affirmative character. Its scope and purpose show, or, at least, tend to show, *by direct proof,* that the school system of Massachusetts is not an anti-Christian, nor an un-Christian system. But there is still another mode of proof. The truth of a proposition may be established, by showing the falsity or absurdity of all conflicting propositions. So far as this method can be applied to moral questions, its aid may safely be invoked here.

What are the other courses, which the State of Massachusetts might adopt or sanction, in relation to the education of its youth? They are these four:—

1. It might establish schools, but expressly exclude all religious instruction from them,—making them merely schools for secular instruction.

2. It might adopt a course, directly the reverse of this. It might define and prescribe a system of religion for the schools, and appoint the teachers and officers, whose duty it should be to carry out that system.

3. It might establish schools by law, and empower each religious sect, whenever and wherever it could get a majority, to determine what religious faith should be taught in them. And,

4. It might expressly disclaim and refuse all interference with the education of the young, and abandon the whole work to the hazards of private enterprise, or to parental will, ability, or caprice.

1. A system of schools from which all religious instruction should be excluded, might properly be called un-Christian,

or, rather, non-Christian, in the same sense in which it could be called non-Jewish, or non-Mahomedan; that is, as having no connection with either. I do not suppose a man can be found in Massachusetts, who would declare such a system to be his first choice.

2. Were the State to establish schools, and prescribe a system of religion to be taught in them, and appoint the teachers and officers to superintend it, could there be any better definition or exemplification of an Ecclesiastical Establishment? . . .

For any human government, then, to attempt to coerce and predetermine the religious opinions of children, by law, and contrary to the will of their parents, is unspeakably more criminal than the usurpation of such control over the opinions of men. The latter is treason against truth; but the former is sacrilege. As the worst of all crimes against chastity are those which debauch the infant victim before she knows what chastity is; so the worst of all crimes against religious truth, are those which forcibly close up the avenues, and bar the doors, that lead to the forum of reason and conscience. The spirit of ecclesiastical domination, in modern times, finding that the principles of men are too strong for it, is attempting the seduction of children. Fearing the opinions that may be developed by mature reflection, it anticipates and forestalls those opinions; and seeks to imprint, upon the ignorance and receptiveness of childhood, the convictions which it could never fasten upon the minds of men in their maturity. . . .

3. As a third method, the government might establish schools by law, and empower each religious sect, whenever and wherever it could get a majority, to determine what religious faith should be taught in them.

Under such a system, each sect would demand that its own faith should be inculcated in all the schools;—and this, on the clear and simple ground that such faith is the only true one. Each differing faith, believed in by all the other sects, must, of course, be excluded from the schools;—and this, on the equally clear and simple ground, that there can be but one true faith; and which that is, has already been determined, and is no longer an open question. Under such a system, it will not suffice to have the Bible in the schools, to speak for itself. Each sect will rise up and virtually say, "Although the Bible from Genesis to Revelation is in the schools, yet its true meaning and doctrines are not there; Christianity is not there, unless our commentary, our creed, or our catechism, is there also. A revelation from God is not sufficient. Our commentary, or our teacher, must go with it, to reveal what the revelation means. . . . Your schools may be like the noble Bereans, searching the Scriptures daily, but unless the result of those searchings have our countersign and endorsement, those schools are un-Christian and anti-Christian."

Now, it is almost too obvious to be mentioned, that such a claim as the above, reduces society at once to this dilemma: If one religious sect is authorized to advance it, for itself, then all other sects are equally authorized to do the same thing, for themselves. The right being equal among all the sects, and each sect being equally certain and equally determined; what shall be done? Will not each sect, acting under religious impulses,—which are the strongest impulses that ever animate the breast of man,—will not each sect do its utmost to establish its supremacy in all the schools? Will not the heats and animosities engendered in families, and among neighbors, burst forth with a devouring fire, in the primary, or district school meetings; and when the inflammable materials of all the district meetings are gathered together in the town meeting, what can quell or quench the flames, till the zealots, themselves, are consumed in the conflagration they have kindled? Why would not all those machinations and oppressions be resorted to, in order to obtain the ascendancy, if religious proselytism should be legalized in the schools, which would be resorted to, as I have endeavored, in a preceding part of this report, to explain, if political proselytism were permitted in the schools? . . .

4. One other system,—if it may be so called,—is supposable; and this exhausts the number of those which stand in direct conflict with ours. It is this: Government might expressly disclaim and refuse all interference with the education of the young, abandoning the whole work to the hazards of private enterprise, or to parental will, ability, or caprice. . . .

* * *

If, then, a government would recognize and protect the rights of religious freedom, it must abstain from subjugating the capacities of its children to any legal standard of religious faith, with as great fidelity as it abstains from controlling the opinions of men. It must meet the unquestionable fact, that the old spirit of religious domination is adopting new measures to accomplish its work,—measures, which, if successful, will be as fatal to the liberties of mankind, as those which were practised in by-gone days of violence and terror. These new measures are aimed at children instead of men. They propose to supersede the necessity of subduing free thought, *in the mind of the adult*, by forestalling the development of any capacity of free thought, *in the mind of the child*. They expect to find it easier to subdue the free agency of children, by binding them in fetters of bigotry, than to subdue the free agency of men, by binding them in fetters of iron. For this purpose, some are attempting to deprive children of their right to labor, and, of course, of their daily bread, unless they will attend a government school, and receive its sectarian instruction. Some are attempting to withhold all means, even of secular education, from the poor, and thus punish them with ignorance, unless, with the secular knowledge which they desire, they will accept theological knowledge which they condemn. Others, still, are striving to break down all free Public School systems, where they exist, and to prevent their establishment, where they do not exist, in the hope, that on the downfall of these, their system will succeed. The sovereign antidote against these machinations, is, Free Schools for all, and the right of every parent to determine the religious education of his children.

This topic invites far more extended exposition; but this must suffice. In bidding an official Farewell to a system, with which I have been so long connected, to which I have devoted my means, my strength, my health, twelve years of time, and, doubtless, twice that number of years from what might otherwise have been my term of life, I have felt bound to submit these brief views in its defence. In justice to my own name and memory; in justice to the Board of which I was originally a member, and from which I have always sought counsel and guidance; and in justice to thou-

sands of the most wise, upright, and religious-minded men
in Massachusetts, who have been my fellow-laborers in ad-
vancing the great cause of Popular Education, under the
auspices of this system, I have felt bound to vindicate it
from the aspersions cast upon it, and to show its consonance
with the eternal principles of equity and justice. I have felt
bound to show, that, so far from its being an irreligious, an
anti-Christian, or an un-Christian system, it is a system
which recognizes religious obligations in their fullest extent;
that it is a system which invokes a religious spirit, and can
never be fitly administered without such a spirit; that it
inculcates the great commands, upon which hang all the
law and the prophets; that it welcomes the Bible, and therefore welcomes all the doctrines which the Bible really contains, and that it listens to these doctrines so reverently,
that, for the time being, it will not suffer any rash mortal
to thrust in his interpolations of their meaning, or overlay
the text with any of the "many inventions" which the heart
of man has sought out. It is a system, however, which leaves
open all other means of instruction,—the pulpits, the Sun-
day schools, the Bible classes, the catechisms, of all denominations,—to be employed according to the preferences of
individual parents. It is a system which restrains itself from
teaching, that what it does teach is all that needs to be
taught, or that should be taught; but leaves this to be decided by each man for himself, according to the light of
his reason and conscience; and on his responsibility to that
Great Being, who, in holding him to an account for the
things done in the body, will hold him to the strictest account for the manner in which he has "trained up" his children.

Such, then, in a religious point of view, is the Massachusetts system of Common Schools. Reverently, it recognizes
and affirms the sovereign rights of the Creator; sedulously
and sacredly it guards the religious rights of the creature;
while it seeks to remove all hinderances, and to supply all
furtherances to a filial and paternal communion between
man and his Maker. In a social and political sense, it is a
Free school system. It knows no distinction of rich and poor,
of bond and free, or between those who, in the imperfect
light of this world, are seeking, through different avenues, to

reach the gate of heaven. Without money and without price, it throws open its doors, and spreads the table of its bounty, for all the children of the State. Like the sun, it shines, not only upon the good, but upon the evil, that they may become good; and, like the rain, its blessings descend, not only upon the just, but upon the unjust, that their injustice may depart from them and be known no more.